I Am of the Tribe of Judah

Jewish Latin America Series
ILAN STAVANS, SERIES EDITOR

The Jewish Latin America Series, relaunched in 2024, will introduce Jewish Latin American culture to a broad English-language readership. Through high-caliber translations as well as original English-language editions, it aims to open up a field of study by publishing classics as well as contemporary novels, memoirs, biographies, story collections, poetry, and anthologies. The series will map out the extraordinary creativity of the Jewish community in Latin America, from colonial times to the present, in a region far more diverse than is usually imagined.

Also available in the Jewish Latin America Series:

Yiddish South of the Border: An Anthology of Latin American Yiddish Writing, edited by Alan Astro
Like a Bride and Like a Mother by Rosa Nissán
Secrecy and Deceit: The Religion of the Crypto-Jews by David M. Gitlitz
The Martyr: Luis de Carvajal, A Secret Jew in Sixteenth-Century Mexico by Martin A. Cohen
Losers and Keepers in Argentina: A Work of Fiction by Nina Barragan
The Collected Stories of Moacyr Scliar by Moacyr Scliar
Passion, Memory and Identity: Twentieth-Century Latin American Jewish Women Writers edited by Marjorie Agosín
The Book of Memories by Ana María Shua, translated by Dick Gerdes
The Jewish Gauchos of the Pampas by Alberto Gerchunoff

I Am *of the* Tribe of Judah

Poems from Jewish Latin America

Edited by Stephen A. Sadow

Introduction by Ilan Stavans

UNIVERSITY OF NEW MEXICO PRESS | ALBUQUERQUE

Printed in the United States of America

ISBN 978-0-8263-6578-1 (paper)
ISBN 978-0-8263-6579-8 (ePub)
ISBN 978-0-8263-6639-9 (webPDF)

Library of Congress Control Number: 2024933540

Founded in 1889, the University of New Mexico sits on the traditional homelands of the Pueblo of Sandia. The original peoples of New Mexico—Pueblo, Navajo, and Apache—since time immemorial have deep connections to the land and have made significant contributions to the broader community statewide. We honor the land itself and those who remain stewards of this land throughout the generations and also acknowledge our committed relationship to Indigenous peoples. We gratefully recognize our history.

Cover art by Ana Wien, resins and pigments on canvas, 100 × 150 cm
Designed by Felicia Cedillos
Composed in Adobe Jenson Pro

For Ricardo Feierstein

Contents

Editor's Note

I invite the reader to partake in the Jewish poetry of Latin America. It is tragic and hopeful, expansive, and involved in the minutiae of everyday life. The Holocaust is a recurrent theme, as is exile and political turmoil. The poets who shape it are romantics, political thinkers, and mystics. On display is a strong pride in being Jewish.

I Am of the Tribe of Judah has allowed me the fortune of discovering extraordinary poets. It has also given me the chance to work with friends. Of the poets and translators, I can count many as personal friends and acquaintances. In fact, my career developed with the support of these friends. I learned from Ricardo Feierstein the importance of publishing Jewish books for those who need to read them. As editor of Editorial Milá and Acervo Cultural Editores in Buenos Aires, Feierstein published more than three hundred volumes on Jewish themes—novels, poetry collections, Holocaust memoirs, philosophy, and humor. During each of my visits to Buenos Aires, he would give me copies of the books.

From Isaac Goldemberg I learned to create anthologies, to look in every direction to find relevant texts, and to ask people to share their works. With Isaac watching over me, I guest edited an issue of the journal *Brújula/Compass* that includes works by Ilan Stavans, Ruth Behar, Marjorie Agosín, and Alicia Borinsky, all of whom became longtime friends.

On July 4, 1994, I sat in the second-floor office of Anita Weinstein in the AMIA (Argentine Israelite Mutual Association) overlooking Pasteur Street in Buenos Aires. Exactly two weeks later I was back in Boston when I learned that a car bomb had completely destroyed the AMIA building, killing eighty-five and wounding three hundred. Anita Weinstein was elsewhere and survived, but her secretary Marta Strier, whom I had met, died that day. I, like so many others, felt shock and intense anger. That day I vowed to dedicate my career to making the work of Latin American Jewish poets, writers, and artists better known, especially in English-speaking countries.

J. Kates, a high-school friend and award-winning translator, helped me make this happen. Over the years he has taught me how to be a literary translator. We have collaborated multiple times. When he and I render a poem in English, first I prepare a rough draft, then we go over it line by line, at times spending an hour on a single phrase. We have been doing this for thirty-five years and have published our collaborative efforts in a steady stream of literary magazines and in seven published books. Many of these cotranslations are featured in *I Am of the Tribe of Judah*.

In 1997 Ilan Stavans, then editor of the first epoch of the Jewish Latin America Series of the University of New Mexico Press, recruited me to assemble a book of essays by Jewish Latin American writers. The result was *King David's Harp* (1999). I got to know Moacyr Scliar, Marcos Aguinis, and José Kozer. The volume subsequently won the National Jewish Book Award for Autobiography-Memoir. I then translated for the series *Mestizo* (2001) by Ricardo Feierstein, *The Algarrobos Quartet* (2003) by Gerardo Goloboff, and the autobiography of Auschwitz survivor Charles Papiernik (2006).

Isaac Goldemberg asked me to edit an issue of the *Revista Hostosiana / Hostos Review*, a bilingual journal he directed for the City University of New York. It was 2005. This time the number of writers grew exponentially. Bringing together one hundred Latin American writers for this 425-page anthology resulted in long-term relationships with many of them.

Argentine artist Perla Bajder and curator Irene Jaievsky asked me in 2009 to help in creating fourteen large (28" × 11") artist's books. Each book was composed of a poem by a Latin American Jewish poet and a translation I did with J. Kates, both accompanied by an original artwork by a Latin American Jewish artist that reacted directly to the poem. The collection was first exhibited at the Jewish Museum of Buenos Aires in 2010, then traveled to fourteen presentation sites in Mexico City, New York, Arizona, Texas, Massachusetts, and Colorado, after which the collection of art books was donated to the Schusterman Center for Jewish Studies at the University of Texas-Austin, and then moved to the university's world-famous Blanton Museum.

I moved online to reach a larger audience. On the website https://www.latinjewisharts.northeastern.edu, readers can access "A Voice among the

Multitudes," which contains translations of the works of thirteen poets, the twenty-fifth anniversary edition of *We, The Generation in the Wilderness* by Ricardo Feierstein, and artworks and interviews with thirteen Argentine Jewish writers and artists. Likewise, my weekly blog, https://jewishlatinmerica.com, showcases creative work and social commentary presented in a bilingual format. Its 400 entries have received more than 100,000 hits from 103 countries and territories.

All this is a way to map out how this anthology, *I Am of the Tribe of Judah*, came about. The vast majority of the poets are represented by a single poem, while others' oeuvres are shown with two or three poems. Biographical headnotes precede each section, offering useful information, including career benchmarks and significant book titles. The translators' names and the original language from which they translated follow each poem. In the back of the book there is also a list of translators, a list of poets, and a guide to titles and first lines.

Acknowledgments

The editorial staff at the University of New Mexico Press is wonderful to work with. I thank Senior Acquisitions Editor Michael Millman for his unrelenting excitement about the project and his straightforward and fruitful advice; Editorial, Design, and Production Manager James Ayers for his help in creating such a beautiful book; and Editor Anna Pohlod for her precision, dedication, and good humor.

Introduction

Swaying To and Fro

ILAN STAVANS

Doubt is one of the names of intelligence.

—JORGE LUIS BORGES

1.

By nature, Jewish poetry is inhabited by a deep sense of ambivalence: on one hand, poets long to feel at home wherever they are situated; and on the other, they see themselves as outsiders, traveling from one diaspora to another. It's an impossible duality. The classic poem accounting for this division is by the medieval Spanish poet Yehuda Halevi, author of the philosophical disquisition *Sefer ha-Kuzari* (The Book of Khazars), who was born in Toledo but throughout his life longed to return to the Holy Land, and, indeed, died on a boat en route to Jerusalem in 1141 as the crusades were under way. "My heart is in the East, and I am in the faraway West" is Halevi's most famous line. He adds: "How can I savor food? . . . How might I render my vows and bonds, while Zion is under the might of Edom, and I am in Arab bondage?" Yet what gives Halevi a sense of mission, what allows him freedom, is the writing of poetry. Through poetry he maps out his condition.

As a mantra, Halevi's dilemma is enlightening. Alienated as they might feel, Jewish poets write about all sorts of things: joy and loss, the search for meaning and the minutiae of everyday life. In Latin America, where poets are perceived as royalty (think of José Martí, Gabriela Mistral, Jorge Luis Borges, Alfonsina Storni, Pablo Neruda, César Vallejo, and Octavio Paz, to name only a few), this push and pull is crystalized in superb verses written by Jewish poets over the centuries. These writers feel compelled to examine their bifurcation with gusto, using intelligence—actually, doubt—as a tool to investigate its universality. At times they write from the fringes; at others, from the mainstream. Either way, they have established a dialogue with each other and with readers the world over and are embraced by a large public: Carlos Grünberg, Lázaro Liacho, and César Tiempo, for instance, commanded enormous attention in Argentina in the first half of the twentieth century; Angelina Muñiz-Huberman is a member of the Academia Mexicana de las Letras. Héctor Yánover was the host of the popular TV show *La librería en su casa* (The Bookstore in Your Home). Juan Gelman was awarded the Cervantes Prize, the most prestigious of the Spanish language. Carlos Jacobo Levy directed Radio Nacional in Mendoza, Argentina. And Manuela Fingueret was director of Radio Jai, the most important Jewish radio station in Latin America. In other words, the poetic tradition they represent explores the divided heart through a cosmopolitan lens.

This anthology provides a generous sampler of that tradition. It collects nearly a hundred poems written from the mid-sixteenth century through the second decade of the twenty-first, written in an assortment of languages, including Spanish, Portuguese, Ladino, Yiddish, Hebrew, English, and Casteidish, the hybrid of Yiddish and Spanish used by immigrants to Argentina. Stephen A. Sadow ought to be commended for being a pathfinder. He has gathered in this anthology an astonishingly rich assortment of voices. To appreciate the nuances generated by the double consciousness at the heart of these poems, it is vital to see this poetic tradition in historical context. Jews have been chroniclers of daily life in Latin America ever since the region entered modernity; that is, starting at the moment when the European and Indigenous civilizations first saw each other face to face. The date was October 12, 1492, just a few months after the Alhambra Decree went into effect in Spain, expelling the Jews from Iberian lands, de facto ending the centuries-old period known as La Convivencia, or the Coexistence, in which the three Abrahamic religions, Judaism, Christianity, and Islam, coexisted more or less harmoniously. Columbus and his expedition arrived in Hispaniola, the island shared today by Haiti and the Dominican Republic, on three ships. His crew included several members known to have been conversos; that is, individuals who, willingly or otherwise, had converted to Christianity, or their families had, to avoid persecution from the Holy Office of the Inquisition.

One of those crew members was Luis de Torres (née Yosef ben Ha-Levi Haivri), who, as Columbus records in his maritime diary, was his interpreter. He knew Hebrew, Arabic, and Chaldaic. Although de Torres didn't write poetry, per se, whatever references we have of his endeavors are splendidly poetic. According to Columbus, de Torres addressed the natives in San Salvador in Hebrew, believing they were descendants of the Lost Tribes of Israel. The admiral also stated that de Torres called the first turkey he came across—a bizarre bird, never seen before by Europeans—a *tukki,* which is parrot in biblical Hebrew. The story is false, because etymologically the word *turkey* comes from a shortening of *turkey-cock* and *turkey-hen,* the original names of the guinea fowl that were imported into Europe from Turkey. Still, after Columbus returned to Europe, de Torres apparently stayed in the Spanish settlement in La Navidad in Hispaniola and spoke disparagingly of the Catholic faith. This, according to some historians, is unquestionable proof of his troubled relationship with Catholicism.

Thus began the first wave of Jewish immigration to the Americas. This wave is frequently described as Sephardic, meaning from Sepharad, as Spain is called in the Hebrew Bible. A few of those who were part of it descend from Ottoman immigrants who crossed the Atlantic Ocean at the beginning of the twentieth century, while others are Mizrahim, Levantine Jews whose ancestry goes back to the Babylonian exile in the year 70 CE and whose ancestors lived in Baghdad, Cairo, Alexandria, and other Arab cities. I will talk about the "other" Sephardim later. For now it is essential to emphasize that the conversos in Columbus's fleet, and others who came to the Americas later, saw the journey as a search for a safe haven from the Inquisition, even though the Holy Office eventually expanded into New Spain and the Province of Peru, what is today Mexico and Peru, and, to a lesser extent, other cities of the New World.

It is estimated that between fifty thousand and two hundred thousand Jews departed from Spain due to the Alhambra Decree. Conversos were viewed with suspicion by the mainstream in Spain and the colonies, accused of not having *pureza de sangre* (purity of blood). The distrust was due to the belief among gentiles that more than a few individuals had only superficially transformed into full-fledged Christians, while the majority remained loyal to their ancestral religion and continued to practice it in secret through all kinds of subterfuges. Another name for conversos was *criptojudíos* (Crypto-Jews), meaning secret Jews. Yet one more was *Marranos*, Spanish for pigs. And then there were *Cristianos nuevos* (New Christians), descendants from conversos who saw themselves as fully Catholic and thoroughly disliked being compared to conversos, whom they considered hypocrites.

It isn't surprising that the conversos were prone to literature. There was an outburst of converso writing—novels, memoirs, poems—from the late fifteenth century onward. It took place in the Spanish diaspora: Italy, Greece, the Netherlands, North Africa, and the Americas. Even though the colonies were considered to be less cultured than Spain, there was a small yet avid readership in them. Picaresque Spanish narratives like Fernando de Rojas's *La Celestina* and the anonymously written *Lazarillo de Tormes*, infused with coded messages by their Crypto-Jewish authors, circulated secretly in the New World, despite being censored by the Inquisition for alleged heresy. Even *Don Quixote de La Mancha*, published in two parts in 1605 and 1615 and a popular book in the colonies, was considered to be imbued with a Marrano sensibility because one of Cervantes's ancestors was Jewish.

Converso poets appear right from the beginning in this collection. Leonor de Carvajal and her brother Luis de Carvajal the Younger, also known as Joseph Lumbroso and "El Iluminado," arrived from Spain in their teens under the tutelage of their uncle, Luis de Carvajal the Elder, governor of the northern state of Nuevo León and a brazen politician known as *el pacificador de los indios* (the pacifier of the Indians). Carvajal the Younger's odyssey is of special significance. Rediscovering his Judaism after rejecting the Catholic education he had been raised with, Carvajal the Younger proselytized among the small converso community in various places in New Spain. Discovering his activities, the Holy Office arrested him along with his mother and sister. Prison radicalized him even more. He was released, but the Inquisition followed his activities closely and was thus able to identify many of his followers. It was during this period that Carvajal the Younger wrote what is believed to be the first Jewish autobiography ever composed in the Americas. He was then caught again and, along with his mother and sister, was burned at the stake in 1596 in an auto-da-fé in Plaza del Quemadero, a site in downtown Mexico City today near the Palacio de Bellas Artes and Alameda Central. The Mexican painter Diego Rivera, who considered himself a descendant of conversos, includes references to it in his celebrated mural *Sueño de una tarde dominical en la Alameda Central*

(Dream of a Sunday Afternoon in Alameda Central Park), which he painted in 1946 and 1947 and is currently at the Museo Mural Diego Rivera. The Carvajal the Younger manuscript, kept in Mexico's National Archives, disappeared mysteriously in the 1930s. It was rediscovered in 2018 as it was about to be auctioned at Sotheby's. It was repatriated and is currently housed in a museum run by Mexico's Jewish community.

Although Carvajal the Younger didn't consider himself a poet—what mattered to him was being a later-day biblical prophet—he left behind a treasure trove of, among other items, liturgical chants known as *alabanzas*. These are prayers that look at the believer in God as an imperfect creature. Carvajal's poems relish the Almighty as a source of constant comfort. Leonor de Carvajal y Andrade, Carvajal's younger sister, was also imprisoned by the Inquisition and similarly composed religious chants to the Almighty. While these exercises might not on their face be of extraordinary artistic value, they are a testament to the fervor conversos held inside, what the sayings of the famous Jewish exegete Bahya ben Yosef ibn Paquda refer to as "the duties of the heart."

Perhaps the most controversial—and epigrammatic—sonnet composed by a converso is "Mileno vs. Apolindo," attributed to Juan Bautista Corvera, born in Toledo, Spain. He immigrated to the Province of Peru in his twenties and later went to New Spain and was a vicar in Apseo in Guanajuato. Considered the first Spanish-language playwright in the Spanish colonies, he also wrote *villancicos*, *chanzonetas*, and *motetes*, all varieties of songs intended for religious holidays. Corvera discusses heresy, a theme proscribed in converso poetry since its mere enunciation amounted to a confession of concealment. These are the two tercets of "Mileno vs. Apolindo":

> Might the blasphemy you spoke pay off
> when you face the Spirit in Heaven,
> lowering the beauty so exalted,
>
> which, by God's honor, lies on earth,
> thus excusing you for thinking
> that such known truth is uncontested.

In other words, conversos felt like imposters. Indeed, the Sephardic lineage in

Jewish Latin American poetry is colored by a constant sense of masquerading, of being a pretender, an impersonator. This is part of the ambivalence of the push and pull and the quest to put doubt as the gravitational center of the poetic quest. One such case could have been Sor Juana Inés de la Cruz, a fiercely feminist nun who is arguably the most influential poet of the colonial age in Latin America. Her grandmother was Jewish. Was Sor Juana fully aware of her *impureza de sangre?* She writes in her "Soneto 146" (Sonnet #146) about an ostracized life. The first line is "In persecuting me, World, what's your interest?" She goes on to talk about her ordeal as a woman, about seeking enlightenment through the life of the mind while looking at appearances as a form of deceit. Or consider her "Soneto 165" (Sonnet #165), in which Sor Juana describes an elusive shadow—"a fantastic form constrained"—visiting her in her most private moments. Rather than expelling the shadow, she wants it to stay with her.

The mystical trend in Spanish poetry passes through figures like Santa Teresa de Ávila, Fray Luis de León, and San Juan de la Cruz, all known to be New Christians. (In 1986 Catherine Swietlicki wrote an important study about them, *Spanish Christian Cabala.*) In Halevi's *Sefer ha-Kuzari,* one of the characters asks why Jews sway when reading the Bible, to which a rabbi responds: "It is said that it is done in order to arouse natural heat." Conversos thought the conflicted identity that marred them mirrored a higher design. More than a few were interested in mystical—e.g., neo-Platonic—views of the universe in secret coding and numinous visions of the divine. Some used mathematics to decrypt messages of their surroundings that they believed only a small cabal of illuminati could untangle.

That penchant for symbolism is still present today in Jewish Latin American poets who see themselves as belonging to the Sephardic lineage. Arguably the most eminent one and one I hold in high esteem is Angelina Muñiz-Huberman. The daughter of Spanish refugees of the Spanish Civil War, she was raised Catholic although her family was converso. The family immigrated to Mexico when she was a teenager. She converted to Judaism after witnessing several idiosyncratic home rituals (the sweeping of the floor before Shabbat, the cooking of certain recipes before certain dates in the calendar, etc.) typical among Crypto-Jewish families. Aside from being a poet, Muñiz-Huberman is an essayist, novelist, and translator. She has written about almost every aspect of Iberian and Sephardic culture. An example is her poem "Los cabalistas" (The Kabbalists), in which she investigates the passing of knowledge among mystics. "From on high they received the divine voice," she writes, "the spark that kindles the heart." In another one of her poems, "El ojo de la creación" (The Eye of Creation), Muñiz-Huberman eloquently reflects on the ways the world keeps repeating itself since time immemorial. There is a force that "labors and tools," pushing "the hidden river of quiet waters" to persist in its rhythms. That supreme force allows us to see, at every moment, creation being born again. The eye of creation is a useful image to appreciate the role Jewish poets have in naming objects, scenes, and emotions. That, in essence, is what the poets gathered here are after: an eye-witness account of why things are what they are.

There are more than a dozen poets in this collection who explore Sephardic motifs, among them Julia Galimare, Leonor Scliar-Cabral, Juana García Abás, Luis Kleiman, Myriam Moscona, and Ruth Behar. Their quest is to understand the nostalgia for a home from which one's ancestors were expelled and also to appreciate the hidden forces that shape life in unrecognized ways. Equally significant is the magnetic attraction to mysticism. Aside from Muñiz-Huberman, others such as Jenny Asse Chayo, Aída Gelbtrunk, José Luis Fariñas, Moacir Amâncio, and Isaac Goldemberg delve into this source. Mystical figures like Abraham Abulafia, Isaac Abulafia, and Judah Loew ben Bezalel, the Maharal of Prague, are inspirations through their teachings and writings. Likewise, the ten Sephirot, golems, and concepts like Gilgul, Adam Kadmon, Tzimtzum, Tikkun Olam, and especially the female aspect of the divine known as Shekinah, make recurrent appearances in Jewish Latin American poetry. One of the most popular scholars among Latin American poets is German-Israeli scholar Gershom Scholem, who opened up the field of Kabbalah and Jewish mysticism in the mid-twentieth century through his book *Major Trends in Jewish Mysticism* (1941). A few of these poets are also attracted to Indigenous shamanism and other spiritual leanings in Latin America. Aiming for a syncretic approach in their verses, they juxtapose these two elements, Kabbalistic mysticism and Indigenous shamanism, to generate enthralling results.

It is a common misconception to expect that conversos in general, and converso poets, communicate in Ladino. Other names for this hybrid Jewish language are *judezmo* and *judeo-español*. Like Yiddish, which was originally a mix of Hebrew and German, Ladino resulted from the intermingling of Hebrew and Spanish. How many Sephardic Jews used Ladino before the expulsion is unknown. However, we know it was widely used in the Ottoman Empire, which started at the end of the thirteenth century in Anatolia, today Turkey, spread to the Balkans, Greece, Northern Africa, and the Middle East, and crumbled six hundred years later around the First World War. There was an orchestrated effort in the second half of the nineteenth century, orchestrated by intellectuals and educators, to transform Ladino from a language written in Hebrew characters to one using a Romanized alphabet. This was done so that the Sephardic communities in the Ottoman Empire would become modern. As part of this effort, large portions of the Ladino-speaking Jewish communities in the region learned French, the fashionable cultural language at the time, which for many became their de facto means of communication.

There was no Ladino poetry in Latin America in the colonial period; all the poetry written by Sephardic authors is written in Spanish. Ladino would not become a poetic language until Ottoman Jews from Syria, Lebanon, Turkey, and Greece emigrated to the New World to escape poverty under Ottoman rule. They brought this hybrid tongue to Latin America. Several poets have continued the tradition of writing in Ladino. One of my favorites is Myriam Moscona, also from Mexico, whose parents were from Sofia, Bulgaria. Moscona learned Ladino at home, mostly through her grandmother. She wrote an autobiography that focuses on that experience called *Tela de sevoya* (Onion Cloth). Along with scholar Jacobo Sefamí, she edited the anthology *Por mi boka* (Through My Mouth). It is significant that her collection of poems *Ansina* (Thus), fully written in Ladino, comes with a glossary in the book's end matter, as if Moscona wants no aspect of the poetry to be misunderstood. Like all writers, she personalizes the language, at times also combining words or inventing new ones. It is, of course, her prerogative: poets manufacture their own vocabulary.

Another Latin American poet also passionate about Ladino is Argentina's Juan Gelman, who, as I mentioned, received the Cervantes Prize, the most prestigious in the Spanish language. In the words of King Juan Carlos when he presented him with the prize, Gelman's poetry is defined by its "strength, sincerity, and spontaneity." His poems are confessional but never melodramatic or even solipsistic. Like César Vallejo, Pablo Neruda, Roque Dalton, Claribel Alegría, and other ideologically engaged poets from Latin America, Gelman speaks truth to power. Born in Buenos Aires of Ashkenazi immigrants, Gelman was jailed in the sixties during the Dirty War because of his participation in the seditious paramilitary group Montoneros. In his poems he embraces experimentalism of all kinds. At times he breaks away from standard grammatical structures, while at others he uses strict rhythmical forms. His poetry is of a syntactically fanciful type, accompanied by unconventional Emily Dickinson–like punctuation, and his passion for Ladino belongs to that playful spirit. Gelman taught himself the language to write his book *Dibaxu*, which was written between 1983 and 1985. The poems in it are spare, almost telegraphic. They are about love, which is an ongoing theme with Gelman, but also about longing for a deeper connection to time.

2.

The colonial period in Latin America is said to have lasted more than three centuries, from 1523 when Hernán Cortés conquered the city of Tenochtitlán until 1810 when the first independence movement took shape in Mexico. This movement was led by a priest, Miguel Hidalgo y Costilla, a freedom fighter who was accused by the Holy Office of the Inquisition of being a Judaizer. The movement created a domino effect that defined the nineteenth century as the age in which emerging Latin American nations, inspired by the political and social ideals of the American Revolution of 1776 and the French Revolution of 1789, sought to break their ties with Europe. By the time Mexico became an autonomous country in 1810, followed by Argentina in 1821, the vast majority of conversos, it seems, had been erased by the tides of history.

The second poetic lineage in Jewish Latin American poetry is Ashkenazic in origin; that is, from Eastern Europe. It came about with the immigrant wave to Argentina, but also to other parts of Latin America at the end of the nineteenth century. Yiddish-speaking shtetl dwellers sought to escape poverty and anti-Semitism in what was known then as the Pale of Settlement, a region encompassing parts of today's Russia as well as Poland, Ukraine, Lithuania, and Belarus. At the time a number of governments in the Americas were eager to populate rural regions. Opening the doors to white Europeans was, shamefully, part of a project to decrease the relevance of the Indigenous population in the region, which they perceived to be awkward and primitive. First and foremost, the Jewish immigrants went to Argentina.

It was an auspicious moment. Sponsored by philanthropic organizations like the Alliance Israélite Universelle and individuals such as the German Jewish businessman and financier Baron Maurice de Hirsch, these individuals and organizations sought alternatives for poor Eastern European Jews to Palestine and the United States. The location in Argentina where Baron de Hirsch and others acquired land was in the Pampas, on the border with Brazil and Uruguay. The Argentine government wanted to ostracize and even eliminate the gaucho population in the country. These skilled cowboys were seen by the Buenos Aires political elite as an impediment in making Argentina a modern country. One of the architects of that effort to whiten the population was Domingo Faustino Sarmiento, a totemic political figure in Argentina and the author of the classic book *Facundo: Civilización y barbarie* (Facundo: Civilization and Barbarism) (1845). In it Sarmiento argued that gauchos were vengeful and unpredictable. He made a gaucho typology—the gaucho singer, the bad gaucho, the tracker gaucho, and so on—and proposed causing them to vanish altogether from the nation's landscape for Argentina to become more "civilized," more like modern Europe.

In 1853 President Justo José de Urquiza encouraged establishing these types of agricultural colonies. The first Jewish colony was Moisés Ville, founded in 1889. Within a few years there were other sprawling Jewish agricultural settlements in the Pampas. They were established in the provinces of Buenos Aires, Entre Ríos, and Santa Fe. The most famous colonies were Moisés Ville, Villa Domínguez, Villa Clara, and Villaguay. Others included Lapin, San Gregorio, and Carmel. In 1895 more than 6,000 people identified as Jewish in the area. They were called *colonos*. More than half of them lived in Entre Ríos province. By 1920 there were approximately 150,000 Jews in Argentina. Within a generation, though, a vast number of them moved to urban centers, principally Buenos Aires but also La Plata and other cities. Yiddish was their domestic language. In a comparatively short period of time, newspapers, theater, radio, and books were produced in Yiddish to satisfy the hunger of these immigrants. A group of poets that featured figures like Moyshe Koyfman and Moishe Pinchevsky started what would be seen as a cultural renaissance. In time other Yiddish poets such as Israel Aszendorf became part of this resurgence. Many of these poets had been connected with cultural centers in Europe where Yiddish thrived, such as Warsaw, Vilna, and Odessa, as well as with New York, where another emergent Yiddish-language literature was taking shape.

Pinchevsky is a unique poet in that he stayed in Argentina only temporarily. He returned to Eastern Europe, where he became a card-carrying member of the Communist Party. His antagonism to Soviet ideology eventually landed him in prison. His work was censored. He died in poverty in Kiev. While his odyssey is distinctive, this back and forth was a feature of immigration. The Yiddish-speaking settlers in the Pampas were in constant dialogue with their original homes. The ease of international travel between the two world wars allowed them to wander through several Jewish diasporas.

Arguably the most famous Yiddish *cantautor* was Jevel Katz. Affectionately called Jévele and Kétzele, Jevel Katz was an immensely popular cantautor, a Jewish troubadour in Argentina famous for combining Yiddish and Spanish in humorous songs: tangos, vitalitas, rumbas, rancheras, and fox-trots. Born in Vilna, he immigrated in 1930 to Buenos Aires, where he became a star on stage, in radio, and in concert. Katz toured Argentina's Jewish agricultural colonies like Moisés Ville, as well as Uruguay and Chile. His funeral is said to have been attended by some forty thousand people. In the translation below I have deliberately rendered Katz's Casteidish—the equivalent of Yinglish in the Southern Cone—through a concoction of Yiddish, Spanish, and English. Call it Yingleñol if you wish. Katz's "Moisés Ville," in which he fashions one of the agricultural colonies as a promised land, is a delightfully comedic depiction of Jewish communal life in the agricultural colonies of the Argentina Pampas. This is a stanza:

> In *mitn pueblito* there's a plaza full of trees,
> youth wanders *oif der najt,*
> people say "*buenas noches,*" and the beasts get out,
> and *take,* not once, a *shidaj* comes out from it all—
> in Moisés Ville,
> my little *shteitele,*
> Moisés Ville,
> my beautiful *heimele,*

you're a *yiddishe medine,*
you're the pride of *Argentine,*
Moisés Ville.

As is clear from Katz's humorous meditation, Yiddish became a conduit through which Yiddish immigrants imagined themselves as full-fledged Argentines. The colonos avidly read Sholem Aleichem, I. L. Peretz, and others, but they were fascinated by gauchos singing of life in the Pampas. They were especially tuned to Yiddish theater and paid for traveling troupes all the way from New York to travel to Argentina.

The leading Jewish Argentine intellectual who transitioned from Yiddish to Spanish was Alberto Gerchunoff, famous for his book *Los gauchos judíos de la Pampa* (The Jewish Gauchos of the Pampas), a collection of vignettes he published in 1910 to celebrate Argentina's first one hundred years of independence. He wrote in Spanish because he had fallen in love with *Don Quixote* and because he wanted to express his gratitude to the country that had opened the doors to him and his family. The book is made of picturesque scenes of Jewish life in the agricultural colonies. Gerchunoff believed Argentina was the new Promised Land, where Jews would thrive in an atmosphere of creativity and tolerance.

Two cataclysmic events took place in Jewish life in Latin America in the twentieth century—one roughly at the beginning of the century, the other at the end. The first occurred in Buenos Aires and is known as the Semana Trágica. It took place from January 7 to January 14, 1919. It encompassed a series of anti-immigrant riots and massacres. It has been at times described as a pogrom, although it had a number of facets that also make it a labor dispute led by anarchists, communists, and other ideologically unified groups that opposed immigration laws and sympathized with the populist president Hipólito Irigoyen, known for fanning the flames in time of increasing economic disparity. The exact number of victims is still disputed: a leftist newspaper suggested there were 700 deaths and 2,000 injured. The United States embassy offered a different number: 1,500 dead, "mostly Russians," which was a euphemism for Jews. The physical, social, and psychological effects of the Semana Trágica are explored in a number of Yiddish poems written not only in the aftermath but all the way into the end of the twentieth century. They appeared in pamphlets, periodicals, and were recited aloud in synagogues and theaters. One example is Simón Zeleviansky's "Baym Taykh de la Plata" (By the River Plate), which is structured as an homage to Psalm 137 in the Bible. The poet accuses Argentina of betraying its promises. It tells the country that received him as an immigrant that it is another Babylon and, as a result, "your future and mine diverge."

The most ambitious publishing undertaking in Yiddish in Argentina is Shmuel Rollansky's one hundred–volume anthology *Musterverk fun der yidisher literatur* (Masterworks of Yiddish Literature), published in Buenos Aires in the 1950s. At 31,000 pages and featuring 952 different authors, it is an extraordinary source of unexplored material awaiting careful scholarship. Rollansky, the director of the Buenos Aires branch of the Institute for Jewish Research, saw it as an attempt to counteract the rapidly diminishing landscape of Yiddish after the Holocaust. There are myriad Yiddish poets from Argentina in *Musteverk*. But this multivolume endeavor also showcases the degree to which Yiddish was a conduit for literary explorations in other Latin American countries, including Cuba, Chile, Colombia, and Mexico. A thorough study of this continental effervescence still needs to be done.

Mexican writer Yitzkhok Berliner's work is a lucid example of impressionistic poetry in Yiddish about how immigrants saw the perplexing American reality before their eyes. His book *Shot fun palatsn* (City of Palaces) offers a series of impressions of Mexico and its people: the enormous volcanoes in the capital, the magisterial churches in the countryside, all types of folk characters like the *peladito*, the *escuincle*, and so on. What distinguishes *Shtot fun palatsn* are a series of twelve drawings by Diego Rivera included in the book. How Berliner and Rivera became friends—a poor Yiddish immigrant from Belarus and a distinguished muralist with left-leaning credentials—is a mystery. Rivera didn't speak Yiddish, yet he believed his family descended from conversos.

Another key Yiddish poet from Mexico was Jacobo Glantz. A flamboyant character who was friends with Rivera and his wife Frida Kahlo (his face served as a model for Rivera's portrait of Leon Trotsky, who sought refuge in Mexico from Stalin in 1937), Glantz was a kind of Beatnik avant la lettre, whose free spirit, manifested in his free verse, resulted in a series of poetic explorations about immigration, bohemian life, and politics. Among his artistic endeavors is the book-length poem *Kristobal Kolon* (Christopher Columbus) (1939), in which

Glantz recreates in vivid detail Columbus's impressions of his first voyage across the Atlantic, particularly his encounter with the Indigenous population in Hispaniola. It recalls the poetic explorations by the conversos, although in Glantz's case the narrative is delivered at a historical distance. Glantz imagines de Torres's disappointment at what he sees in Hispaniola.

When Ashkenazic Jews arrived in Latin America, between 1880 and 1930, the continent was in the process of modernization. The aesthetic movement shaping Spanish American letters at the time was appropriately known as *Modernismo.* (It pre-dated European Modernism.) Circumscribed roughly from 1888 to 1915, it sought alignment with ideas and values connected with modern industrial life and took place while Cuba, Puerto Rico, and the Philippines fought for their independence from Spain. It was during Modernismo that streetlights, sewer systems, the telegraph, and refrigerators arrived in Latin America. Tired of Spanish culture, which people perceived as oppressive, writers were looking at France with admiration and trends like Symbolism, Parnassianism, and other fashionable styles became influential.

Ruben Darío's work is an extraordinary lens through which to appreciate Jewish life, including the quandary of Columbus in the New World. In an 1892 poem dedicated to the admiral to commemorate the four hundredth anniversary of Columbus's voyages across the Atlantic, Darío describes Columbus as a farfetched messianic figure. Another germane poem by Darío about Jews, one considerably more explicit, appears in *Cantos de Vida y Esperanza* (Songs of Life and Hope), which includes the poem "Canto a la Argentina," in which he describes Jewish immigration to Argentina at the end of the nineteenth century and in the first decades of the twentieth century. Darío celebrates the Biblical heritage and bucolic present of the colonos of Entre Ríos and Santa Fe. Here is my translation of one of its stanzas:

> Sing, Jews of La Pampa!
> Young men of rude appearance,
> sweet Rebeccas with honest eyes,
> Reubens of long locks,
> patriarchs of white,
> dense, horse-like hair.
> Sing, sing, old Sarahs

and adolescent Benjamins
with the voice of our heart:
"We have found ZION!"

Darío's interest in Jewish themes, while modest, serves as a referendum to understand how the wave of Ashkenazic Jews were perceived by the intellectual and artistic elite.

The central non-Jewish writer interested in *lo judío* (things Jewish), a successor of Modernismo and a full participant in other movements like *Ultraísmo, Vanguardismo*, and *Martínfierrismo*, was Jorge Luis Borges (1899–1986). Unquestionably the most influential writer from the region in the twentieth century, Borges frequently featured Jewish characters in his poetry. Borges has a sonnet dedicated to Spinoza, several poems about Israel as a young independent state, and a long poem about a golem, in which Borges mentions his relationship with the Kabbalah scholar Gershom Scholem. Borges authored a number of celebrated stories with distinct Jewish themes: "El aleph" (The Aleph) about a mysterious object capable of encompassing the entire universe; "Emma Zunz" about a young Jewish woman who takes revenge against her father's killer; "El milagro secreto" (The Secret Miracle), a tribute to Kafka about a Jewish translator who asks God for a secret miracle; and "La muerte y la brújula" (Death and the Compass), a detective story that attempts to solve a series of murders in which all victims are Jewish. A mentee of Gerchunoff (Borges wrote eloquently about him), he composed a variety of poems with Jewish motifs whose impact on future generations, Jewish and non-Jewish, is considerable. He also left his impressions in verse of a couple of trips he made to Israel in the 1970s. And he wrote poetic meditations about mystical symbols, about the connection between Jews and the books. Through his work it is also possible to calibrate the importance of Israel as a young nation (it achieved its independence from British Mandate in 1948), which for scores of Argentine Jews was seen as an opportunity to relocate, since life in Argentina was politically and economically perilous.

Borges wasn't a Zionist, yet he wrote several allegorical poems to Israel. Among the Argentine Jewish poets that Borges befriended was Carlos Grünberg, arguably the most dominant of Jewish authors of his generation and a member, like Borges, of an artistic group known as the *martinfierristas*, named after Argentina's epic *El gaucho Martín Fierro* (The Gaucho Martin Fierro) (1872) by José Hernández. Grünberg was active in the Zionist movement. Right as the Second World War was unfolding, Borges wrote a prologue to Grünberg's collection *Mester de Judería* (Master in Jewish Affairs) (1940), arguing it exemplified "the honor and pain of being Jewish in this incredible, perverse world." His poetry confronted anti-Semitism and articulated the varieties of the Jewish experience, which Grünberg explored by highlighting the tension between German Jews and Yiddish-speaking shtetl dwellers.

Along with Grünberg there are two contemporary intellectuals whose work serves to appreciate the way Jews in Argentina negotiated their environment. One was Lázaro Liacho (1906–1969), a journalist, playwright, essayist, novelist, and poet who explores similar topics in dissimilar ways. A Zionist at heart—far more than Grünberg, who seldom looked beyond his own confines—with a strong Biblical education, Liacho placed his energy in all kinds of literary endeavors: he founded the first Argentine Yiddish daily, *Der tog* (The Day), as well as the weekly *Der Tsionist* (The Zionist). He was involved in Jewish pedagogy and argued for a broader view of Argentine Jewish identity. Yet he, too, saw Argentina as the Promised Land. Later he turned to religious themes as well as anti-Semitism. The other is César Tiempo (1906–1980), a poet, writer, playwright, screenwriter, and journalist. Born Israel Zeitlin in Ukraine, he was brought to Buenos Aires as an infant. In 1924 he became a citizen of Argentina. A member of the aesthetic movement known as *Boedo*, which sought to give voice to the working class, Tiempo wrote sensitively, at times critically, about the Jewish community of Buenos Aires. He became a controversial figure because of his support of Juan Domingo Perón.

3.

While in political terms Latin America was a disjointed front during the Second World War—some countries aligned themselves with the Allies; others professed admiration for Hitler, Stalin, and Mussolini—the Holocaust played a fundamental role in the region. A solid number of survivors arrived during and after the war to Mexico, Cuba, Argentina, Colombia, Ecuador, and elsewhere. Dominican dictator Rafael Trujillo opened his doors to survivors to create a colony in Sosúa, which, although it never had more than five thousand inhabitants, was symbolically important. This happened simultaneously with the so-called Rat Route, through which Nazis such as Adolf Eichmann and Josef Mengele changed their identities and made their way to South America. Jewish poets in Latin America reflected on the tragedy of their relatives in Europe, some dealing with the guilt of not having done enough to save them.

In the works that follow there are abundant poems on the Shoah, from Andrés Berger-Kiss's "No quiero que esta herida sane" (I Don't Want This Wound to Heal), Juana Ciesler's "Su hermano Zalman" (His Brother Zalman), and David Turkeltaub's "Geratevet" (the word means "saved" in Yiddish), to Marjorie Agosín's "Primas" (Cousins), in which her mother murmurs the names of relatives who died in Europe. These poems not only remember the victims but bring their suffering home by equating the odyssey of Jews in the Holocaust to the challenges posed by military dictatorships in Latin America. Indeed, the defining ingredient in twentieth-century Argentina, and to varied extents in other countries of Latin America, is the precariousness of democracy and the recurrent jolts of populism, which often ended up in military regimes. Juan Domingo Perón dominated Argentina's political scene for decades. Fidel Castro did the same in Cuba, Getúlio Vargas in Brazil, General Augusto Pinochet in Chile, and Hugo Chávez in Venezuela, to name only a few. When democracy became a possibility, juntas in Uruguay, Chile, and Argentina took control in a period known as the Guerra Sucia (Dirty War) (1974–1983). Given their need to see themselves as full participants in national life, Jews became active participants in these periods, often on opposing sides of the spectrum: some opposed military juntas and were committed left-wing activists, while others embraced the dictatorial regime. It is symptomatic, for instance, that a portion of the desaparecidos in Argentina in the 1960s and 1970s were Jews. The same happened in Chile. Even when state censorship was at its height, poets like David Turkeltaub sought strategies to chronicle this radicalization.

There is a penchant among the poets included here to use biblical imagery as a mirror of contemporary behavior. Other significant themes are rituals, such as daily prayers, and the celebration of holidays like Rosh Hashana, Yom Kippur, Passover, and Shavuot. The recurrence of these annual cycles allows the poets to reflect on the implacability of time but also on the recognition that our individual behavior is unique only in appearance but in fact repeats patterns that are as old as history. In Leonor Scliar-Cabral's "Shavuot em Granada" (Shavuot in Granada) and Isaac Goldemberg's "Yom Kipur" (Yom Kippur), for example, it is emblematic that such rituals are performed in syncretic—e.g., mestizo—fashion, mixing elements inherited from the immigrant generation with components taken from the native environment. That is one of the most significant lessons to learn here: that survival depends on adaptability. For, in the end, the most stable aspect of the universe is change.

The second catastrophic event that I alluded to before that frames twentieth-century Jewish life in Latin America is the terrorist attack in Buenos Aires against the AMIA, as the city's Jewish community center is known. It happened on July 18, 1994. A van filled with bombs was driven into the AMIA building. The explosion was massive: eighty-five people were killed and three hundred were injured. Orchestrated by Hezbollah operatives, it was a terrifying wake-up call about the widening Middle Eastern conflict between Israel and the Palestinians. Up until then the Jews of Latin America perceived themselves as peripheral to it. The attack instantly changed that view. There are numerous poetic responses to the atrocities, including Carlos Jacobo Levy's "Ay Antonio de nuevo nuevamente pero no" (Ay, Antonio, once again once more but no) and Daniel Chirom's "19 de julio" (July 19) (that is, the day after the attack), written in Spanish. This is a fragment from Chirom's poem:

> Why on this night do shadows take possession of our houses?
> On all other nights, lights illuminate the table,
> but tonight, there is only one candelabra
> so that we remember darkness.
> Why on this night do our hands and tongues tremble?
> [. . .]
> On all other nights, even when death
> steps on our heels,
> we tell the phases of the moon and praise the lion.
> But tonight nobody called at our door,
> and it is already too late for someone to come
> and guide us through the stars.

Another aesthetically different poem by Sigalit Tevet is written in Hebrew. Tevet lists the names of several victims but excludes the names of the various perpetrators, such as the one memorialized in Sidon, Lebanon, by Hezbollah. This, too, is a fragment:

> Ricardo Said,
> who guards the entrance to the building,
> won't witness his daughter
> recite Canto I of *The Gaucho Martín Fierro*
> that evening at a poetry competition:
> "*Aquí me pongo a cantar . . .*"
> There are 300 people injured,
> among them Tía Consuelo,
> whose ears will explode as well
> and shall never pick up
> my phone calls again.
> The echoes are too remote.

It is clear that the AMIA attack is a wound that is still healing. The responses to it range from methodical to emotional.

Death features prominently in the poems collected here in *I Am of the Tribe of Judah*. Andrés Neuman's "Génesis COVID-19" (Genesis COVID-19) is a recreation of the instant in which the Almighty created the world, though now with the perspective of the global pandemic. In "This, in essence, ended . . . ," Sandro Cohen, an American Mexican poet, describes the world *after* his death, which tragically came about from COVID-19 when he was only sixty-seven. César Tiempo laments the death of Chaim Nachman Bialik (who was famous for his poem "In the City of Slaughter" about the pogrom in Kishinev in 1903), while Juan Gelman writes what appears to be his own epitaph. The relationship of Jews with death in and of itself is complex. Poetry is the terrain where its emotional impact is most vividly examined.

A Jewish Latin American poet of astonishing range is Cuba's José Kozer. As the child of parents who immigrated to Havana from Poland and Czechoslovakia, he represents the generation of the children of immigrants. This grants him the perspective of a native. Yet in Kozer's case it is experienced through a prism of detachment. No matter where he finds himself, he constantly feels uncomfortable, disjointed, outside of himself. He is an introspectionist committed to mapping his own personal journey, as a poet, a Jew, and a Cuban. The politics of Castro's Communist revolution along with this inner disquiet eventually forced him out of Cuba and into the United States. Exile, indeed, is a constant in the tradition. Financial insecurities, political strife, as well as an increasing feeling of insecurity have forced many Jewish poets (such as Ariel Dorfman, Isaac Goldemberg, Nora Strejilevich, Marjorie Agosín, Ruth Behar, Andrés Neuman) from the region into exile. Favorite destinations for these poets are Israel, Europe, and the United States, where they have mainly entered academia.

In my mind the two Jewish Latin American poets whose oeuvres represent the apex of this tradition are Alejandra Pizarnik and Gloria Gervitz. Like Kozer, they belong to the generation of the children of immigrants. Pizarnik was born in Buenos Aires to Russian Jewish immigrant parents. She studied philosophy and literature at the University of Buenos Aires before dropping out to pursue painting and her own poetry. In 1960 she moved to Paris, where she befriended Latin American writers such as Octavio Paz, Julio Cortázar, and Silvina Ocampo. Considered one of midcentury Argentina's most powerful and intense lyric poets, Pizarnik counted among her influences Friedrich Hölderlin and, as she wrote in her 1965 essay "La palabra encarnada" (The Incarnate Word), "the suffering of Baudelaire, the suicide of Nerval, the premature silence of Rimbaud, the mysterious and fleeting presence of Lautréamont," and the "unparalleled intensity" of Artaud's "physical and moral suffering." Her themes were cruelty, childhood, estrangement, and death. Pizarnik is superb not only with words but with silences. She reminds me of Sylvia Plath. The raw, crude emotions in her work have attracted new readers since she committed suicide at the age of thirty-six. She is always eager to feel, to experience life in strokes.

Gloria Gervitz, on the other hand, is a patient, exacting poet. She isn't consumed by an inner demon, like Pizarnik seems to me. Born in Mexico in 1943 to Jewish immigrant parents from Ukraine, she spent her life from 1976 weaving together a single magisterial book called *Migraciones* (Migrations), though it changed names over the years. In its stunning poetic breadth, it reminds me of Sor Juana Inés de la Cruz's poem *Primero sueño* (First Dream), an epistemological quest to unravel, during one night, all the secrets of the universe. Just like Sor Juana, whose interests ranged from physics to Greek mythology, from music and cuisine to language and translation (she quoted profusely from Latin authors in the original and incorporated Nahuatl in her *Tocotines*), Gervitz's migrations take her across time and space. Mark Schafer's English-language rendition allows readers to wander with her from the Pale of Settlement, and even before, from biblical and Talmudic times, through Greek and Mexican mythology. Readers are invited to appreciate not only how Jews wander but how they wonder, inquiring about their existence at every step through a series of perplexing questions designed to help them understand their mission in history. As in Borges's all-encompassing Aleph, my impression is that all of Jewish Latin American poetry is contained in *Migrations*, which represents its crowning achievement. This is a book that reminds us the extent to which poetry is an indispensable companion to understand the plight of minorities.

I have spoken about biblical imagery. Another important dimension is the connection with modern-day Israel. Concurrent with the arrival of Jewish immigrant waves to Latin America in the late nineteenth and early twentieth centuries was Zionism as an ideology, pulling people in another geographical direction: Palestine. In the decades since Israel's declaration of independence in 1948, numerous Latin American Jews have made aliyah ("ascendance" in Hebrew) and become Israeli citizens. Entire kibbutzim were identified by their large Argentine, Brazilian, Mexican, and Uruguayan constituencies. A volume of Israeli poetry—in Hebrew—about Latin America still needs to appear. The case of Sigalit Tevet proves that the symbolism embedded in a poem might be subtler and, therefore, nuanced. In contrast, the presence of Israel, in multiple forms, in the poetic tradition represented in this anthology is abundant. Raúl Hecht's "When You Open the Window," dedicated "To Dinorah who is in Israel," and Luisa Futoransky's "Jerusa of My Love" are examples. Yet nostalgia and family ties aren't the only themes. Israel's conflict with the Palestinians and the sales by Israel of weapons to Latin American countries are also addressed.

Needless to say, the poems in *I Am of the Tribe of Judah* come to us in English. This means they have been intervened by translators who have made them comfortable outside their original language. The effort isn't without complications. All translations are interpretations, and all interpretations are biased. It is fitting, in my opinion, that translation is to such an important degree the protagonist here. Jews have wandered from one diaspora to another, and from one language to the next. Similarly, Latin America in its history has been the theater of constant encounters between the Indigenous population and outsiders arriving with a specific vision in mind: to find a new homeland.

As I have tried to make clear, the poets in this collection are active on many levels: a few are short-story writers and novelists, while others are essayists, memorialists, playwrights, and screenwriters. One fundamental aspect to highlight is their own role as translators. Many of the writers in this volume are multilingual and have devoted their energy to translation. Grünberg rendered the poems of Heinrich Heine and Chaim Nachman Bialik into Spanish. Gloria Gervitz was a translator of, among others, Samuel Beckett, Kenneth Rexroth, Rita Dove, and Susan Howe. Sandro Cohen translated parts of Edgar Lee Master's *Spoon River Anthology* and other American poetry. Carlos Jacobo Levy translated *The Gaucho Martín Fierro* into Ladino. Angelina Muñiz-Huberman and her husband, Alberto Huberman, have translated Israel's national poet Yehuda Amichai. Simón Zeleviansky translated sections of *The Arabian Nights* into Yiddish. Sigalit Tevet renders Chilean poets into Hebrew. Others have done the same with Yiddish writers like Isaac Bashevis Singer and with US poets such as Emily Dickinson, Elizabeth Bishop, and Richard Wilbur. This, in any event, is a partial list. Interest in translation—as an intellectual endeavor and as a chance for one's work to become global—is substantial among successive generations of Jewish poets from Latin America. This interest helps us to understand the kinds of reading habits these poets have and their desire to serve as bridges between cultures. Jews have performed such a role since ancient times. The passion for translation, obviously, also spills into the poet's work, making it more cosmopolitan. This, indeed, is a characteristic of this poetic tradition: immersed as it is in the push and pull between belonging and being an outcast, it uses translation as a tool to empathize with others.

Cumulatively the poems gathered in this volume form a kind of midrash of what it means to be a Jewish writer, and specifically the dimensions that Latin America adds to that identity. Where is home? Ambiguity is the rule of the game. In what way am I different from everyone else? The communicating vessels linking these poets to the Jewish and Hispanic traditions, and to world literature in general, are infinite. In a continent ruled by corrupt elites and plagued by lawlessness and a lack of democratic representation, where minorities are often vulnerable to the elements, it is inspiring to see how these poets respond to adversity by writing verses that enunciate the inevitable yet also inject hope in it.

Juan Bautista Corvera (attributed)

Juan Bautista Corvera (1530–?) was born in Toledo, Spain, and moved to Peru at the age of twenty-five and from there to Nueva España, as Mexico was known in colonial times, arguably around 1558. He was accused of being a Judaizer and went through an inquisitorial trial in 1564. Years later he reappeared as a vicar in Apseo in the state of Guanajuato. According to literary historians Amado Alonso and Alfonso Méndez Plancarte, Corvera is considered the first Spanish-language playwright—at least the first known one—in what is Mexico today. He was also a poet known to compose chanzonetas, villancicos, and motetes for a variety of religious holidays. The sonnet "Mileno vs. Apolindo," sometimes attributed to him, tacitly acknowledges the alternative approaches Crypto-Jews in the New World had to their public identity.

MILENO VS. APOLINDO

Might the strongest of forces grant power
to your stolid heart, contrary and fearsome,
and might it make your eyes a partner
in the instruction of moral discernment.

These talents you must espouse in full,
allowing for self-knowledge that is truthful,
bringing in the benefit of alienation,
enticing you to the glories of distrainment.

Might the blasphemy you spoke pay off
when you face the Spirit in Heaven,
lowering the beauty so exalted,

which, by God's honor, lies on earth,
thus excusing you for thinking
that such known truth is uncontested.

—Translated from Spanish by Ilan Stavans

Leonor de Carvajal y Andrade

A younger sister of Luis de Carvajal the Younger, Leonor de Carvajal y Andrade (1573–1596) married Jorge Almeida in 1575 in Portugal and moved to Mexico, where she rediscovered her Jewish faith. Along with her mother, Francisca Nuñez y Carvajal, sister Isabel Rodríguez de Andrada, and brother Luis de Carvajal the Younger, she was burned in an auto-da-fé in Mexico City. She wrote liturgical poems and panegyrics.

FOR ALL WHO TRUST HIM

We sing in joy
in praise of El Señor—
for all who trust Him
are regaled with favor.

We sing in joy
as we await King Josaphat,
who leads with mercy
through days of adversity.
El Señor, divine in majesty,
showers us with praise—
for all who trust Him
are regaled with favor.

Ours is a story of people
traveling across earth
in pursuit of obedience.
The Omnipotent is
our sole, true defender—
for all who trust Him
are regaled with favor.

We sing in joy
as El Señor sends us prophets
whose path we follow
with faith and endurance
as they lead the way—
for all who trust Him
are regaled with favor.

—Adapted from Spanish by Ilan Stavans

Luis de Carvajal the Younger

Luis de Carvajal y de la Cueva the Elder, a Crypto-Jew, was the governor of the northern Mexican state of Nuevo León and was known as "the pacifier of the Indians." He helped his family move to Nueva España, where the Holy Office was known to have a more limited control on people's lives. Luis de Carvajal the Younger (1566–1596) was among them. He reawakened to his ancestral Jewish faith, changed his name to Josef Lumbroso and "El Iluminado," and helped establish a secret community of Crypto-Jews until he was arrested by the Inquisition. He was burned in an auto-da-fé in Mexico City's Plaza del Quemadero. Among his surviving work is what is considered to be the first autobiography by a Jew in the New World, as well as correspondence and panegyrics. His odyssey has been recreated in novels, movies, and historical accounts, including Arturo Ripstein's film *El Santo Oficio* (1975), Martin Cohen's biography *The Martyr* (2001), and Ilan Stavans's graphic novel *El Iluminado* (2012) and journalistic mystery *The Return of Carvajal* (2019).

YOU, WITHOUT YOU

I've sinned, Señor, but not because I've sinned.
I bode farewell to Your love and mercy;
I fear punishment according to my guilt,
and by Your kindness, I hope to be forgiven.

I recant, according to Your patience,
and I am, by my ingratitude, abhorred.
My sin makes it all the more sizable
for You to be worthy to be loved.

If it weren't for You, would I be someone?
And I, from me, without You, could I be freed,
did Your hand not grant me grace?

If not me, Señor, who would love You?
And if not You, who might suffer me?
You, without You, who could grant me guidance?

—Adapted from Spanish by Ilan Stavans

Gonzalo Pérez Ferro

Little is known about Gonzalo Pérez Ferro (1567–?), other than the fact that, along with his wife, Catalina de León, and their son, he was arrested by the Holy Office in Mexico on charges of being a Judaizer in Nueva España. A couple of religious poems written by him survive.

SHEMÁ ISRAEL

Shemá Israel,
Adonay our God,
El Señor is one.
Adonay is my mentor,
plentiful in his power,
placing His left hand over my mind,
His right over my heart.
Shemá Israel,
Adonay our God,
El Señor is one.
As I walk through open fields,
I am nourished.

—Adapted from Spanish by Ilan Stavans

Yitzkhok Berliner

A Yiddish poet who collaborated with Diego Rivera, Yitzkhok Berliner (1899–1967) was born in Lodz, Poland, and is known in Spanish as Isaac. He immigrated to Mexico in 1922, where he at first worked as a peddler. His poetry is found in the anthology *Dray vegn* (1927), which also features work by Jacobo Glantz and Moishe Glikovski. He is best known for his impressionistic, politically conscious volume *Shtot fun palatsn* (1936), with illustrations by Rivera. Berliner was also the author of *Ad mosay* (1941), *Shtil zol zayn* (1948), and *Gezang fun mentsh* (1954). He died in Mexico City.

FROM *POPOCATÉPETL*

Popo—
lying stolid with a plumage of stone,
crying from your body, with a quiet scream,
are thousands of years.

In the bluish dawn of rose,
the sun hides its whitish head
with rainbow stripes,
like a hairband.

Winds—
hidden monsters in the gallop,
throwing themselves onto you, yelling as they pillage,
humming songs and whistling
from unknown lands.

What secrets,
stored in the passing of generations,
are hidden inside you?

What scars,
stapled in blood,
are engraved in individual stones?

Carry me inside your body, Popo,
stone-like,
conveying
your mysteries in my silence.

Popo—
furtive hoary giant,
the sun throws you a ray
in the darkening moments of dusk,
enlightening you fully.

I see in you now
ancient generations gone,
their blood spilled
from your vertebral column.

What plethora of travelers wandered on your silvery skin?
Have you counted their steps?

At your knees
death announces its journey,
and on your back,
this frigid, whitish miracle
pours inscrutability . . .

—Translated from Yiddish by Ilan Stavans

Shloyme Kleinberg

Born in Nowe Bródno, Poland, Shloyme Kleinberg (1878–1947) was a yeshiva student in Warsaw. After meeting novelist Israel Joshua Singer, he started to keep a personal diary, which he kept up until his immigration to Bogotá in 1940. A couple of years after his arrival to Colombia, he met poet León de Greiff, who introduced him to other local writers. He appeared to have traveled to Buenos Aires, where he was said to have had an affair with essayist and translator José Bianco, who was on staff at the literary journal *Sur*. In a relatively short creative period, he wrote sonnets, villancicos, and free verse in Yiddish, as well as short stories. After his suicide his sister disposed of his oeuvre. Only a portion of his personal diary and a few literary samples have survived. He died in Bogotá, Colombia.

IN-BETWEEN QUESTION

Behind is the past, what is seen no more.
Behind is the beginning.

Ahead is the future, what is yet unborn.
Ahead is the end.

Behind is silence.
Ahead is resonance.

Behind is death.
Ahead is birth.

Where am I?

—Translated from Yiddish by Ilan Stavans

Moishe Pinchevsky

Moishe Pinchevsky (1894–1955) was a Yiddish poet, translator, and playwright whose odyssey reflects the turbulence of Jewish life in the first half of the twentieth century. Born in Telenesti, Bessarabia, Pinchevsky studied in a yeshiva at the age of sixteen. His father was a Kabbalist. After 1913 he worked as a cabin boy and visited Argentina, Brazil, and Chile. His poems about gauchos and the agricultural colonies were a result of his trips. He immigrated to Argentina, where he published *Di idishe tseytung* in collaboration with Pinye Katz. His book *Tsvit* (1918), considered among the most important in Argentine Yiddish literature, explains his inclusion in Samuel Rollansky's *Musteverk* in the sections on Argentina. Pinchevsky returned to Bessarabia in 1921. Aside from plays, his works include the books *Lider fun tog* (1932), *Undzere kinder* (1933), and *Dos lebn un der toyt fun vilyam sven* (1935). In 1935 he became a member of the Writers Union of the USSR. Four years later he was arrested under the suspicion of being a foreign agent. He was released and then in 1951 imprisoned again, this time in a labor camp, for "anti-Soviet agitation." He was set free a year before his death in Kyiv, Ukraine.

ARRIVING EARLY

Arriving, so it seems, way too early,
dressed up in tailcoat   and top hat,
I come across a pair of old men,
along with one-two   little children.

Where to find the bride and groom?
Who shall I now be greeting?
Children laughing, being witty,
old men yawning, sneezing.

A feast without in-laws,
and I, arriving way too early,
my song, surging in this hall,
hollow   and empty, is muted.

Just a minute—I shall sing
for the stunning, youthful cook,
her eyes, black and warm,
punch you, nail you down.

Dressed up in tailcoat   and top hat,
I shall hug the comely cook.
For her I will sing my song—
being soft, feeling gentle.

—Translated from Yiddish by Ilan Stavans and Eliezer Nowodworski

Jacobo Glantz

Born in Novovitebsk, Ukraine, into a religious family, Yankev Glantz (1902–1982), better known in Spanish as Jacobo Glantz, attended a variety of schools, in which he learned Russian and Yiddish. He immigrated to Mexico in 1925, where he was employed in a variety of jobs. In 1927 he began writing for *Meksikaner Yiddish Lebn*, and he later served as the literary editor of *Der veg* between 1936 and 1946. He and his wife also owned the restaurant Café Carmel in Zona Rosa. He was a friend of Diego Rivera and Frida Kahlo. In 1939 a fascist group tried to lynch him in downtown Mexico City; the episode is chronicled by his daughter Margo Glantz in her memoir *The Family Tree* (1981). While he was a prolific poet and essayist who wrote in Russian, Yiddish, and Spanish, he is best known for his epic poem *Kristobal Kolon* (1939). A sample of his poetry is featured in the anthology *Dray vegn* (1927), which also includes poetry by Yitzkhok Berliner and Moishe Glokovski.

THE MEANING OF MY LIFE

Over a delicate mesh,
a spider weaves incessantly
a trap for herself.
(A fly flutters above,
not knowing its fate.)
I have also
fallen prey
to the appealing net
of the hours of time.

—Translated from Yiddish by Ilan Stavans

FROM *KRISTOBAL KOLON*, PART II, SECTION 17

And the spies return
from the crevices
of the varied island.
The spies are back
to the pier
where the caravels await.
They wash up their feet
in the refreshing lagoon,
shake off, onto the wind,
the dust on their cloths.
Columbus and his crew
greet them.
De Torre writes down,
from Columbus's hand,
in Latin letters,
a missive to His Spanish Majesty:
—he didn't find
the King, the Almighty,
Señor de Señores,
from the island of Zipangu.
Twelve miles of travel
across the land in the island—
no sign of his "enormous empire."
A village was located,
made of five dozen shacks
resembling *sukkot* in Murcia,
the same provincial style;
huts weaved together over the landscape
through palm leaves;
and a thousand souls

inside those tents:
gigantic men,
their flesh reddened,
decorated, tattooed,
tanned by the wind;
women,
like statues,
shamelessly exposed;
all bronze figures,
svelte like swans;
elastic tights,
like grown palms.

A melancholy moon
shines over the island at night;
the solitude is terrifying—
of icy tombs
in the silent cemeteries
of Old Castile . . .
And crickets sing,
insects vibrate;
mockingbirds whistle
as the springs murmur
and fireflies project themselves
in wolverine eyes.
No gold is abundant
on the hills and amidst the rivers;
yet, according to native promulgations,
gold is found thus,
as are treasures full of pearls
in Bohio Island.
And in the island of Babeka,

cinnamon bushes,
like palms, rise up.
Spices abound:
ginger and saffron,
red pepper,
and piquant roots . . .

—Translated from Yiddish by Ilan Stavans

Jevel Katz

Affectionately called Jévele and Kétzele, Jevel Katz (1902–1940) was an immensely popular cantautor, a Jewish troubadour in Argentina famous for combining Yiddish and Spanish in humorous songs: tangos, vitalitas, rumbas, rancheras, and fox-trots. Born in Vilna, Lithuania, he immigrated to Buenos Aires, Argentina, in 1930, where he became a star on stage, radio, and in concert. Katz toured Argentina's Jewish agricultural colonies like Moisés Ville, as well as Uruguay and Chile. His funeral is said to have been attended by some forty thousand people. In this translation I have deliberately rendered Katz's Casteidish—the equivalent of Yinglish in the Southern Cone—through a concoction of Yiddish, Spanish, and English. Call it Yingleñol.

MOISÉS VILLE

Jews, be happy at this miraculous hour,
in a corner of Argentina, the *moshiach* has arrived!
Here there are no Christians,
nor small- or big-shot Jews,
the *apteker*, the *bañero*, the *comisar*, and the judge—
in Moisés Ville,
my little *shteitele*,
Moisés Ville,
my beautiful *heimele*,
you're a *yiddishe medine*,
you're the pride of *Argentine*,
Moisés Ville.

In *mitn pueblito* there's a plaza full of trees,
youth wanders *oif der najt*,
people say "*buenas noches*," and the beasts get out,
and *take*, not once, a *shidaj* comes out from it all—
in Moisés Ville,
my little *shteitele*,
Moisés Ville,
my beautiful *heimele*,
you're a *yiddishe medine*,
you're the pride of *Argentine*,
Moisés Ville.

A radio *shpiels* tangos, and the public takes a stroll,
wives tell *mayses* about what in *shtetls* occur,
who's having a *tnoyim*, where there'll be a *bris*,
and who on *fraytik* is burning a knish—
in Moisés Ville,

my little *shteitele,*
Moisés Ville,
my beautiful *heimele,*
you're a *yiddishe medine,*
you're the pride of *Argentine,*
Moisés Ville.

In the plaza stands a *mentch,* a *pundik* no doubt,
with wide *bombaches,* with *alpargatas* on his feet,
through the *bigotes* he whistles a Spanish *lid,*
you can be sure the *criollo* is a *yid*—
in Moisés Ville,
my little *shteitele,*
Moisés Ville,
my beautiful *heimele,*
you're a *yiddishe medine,*
you're the pride of *Argentine,*
Moisés Ville.

—Translated from Casteidish by Ilan Stavans

Moishe Glikovski

Along with Yitzkhok Berliner and Jacobo Glantz, Polish-born Moishe Glikovski (1904–?) was one of three poets who contributed to the anthology *Dray vegn* (1927). Scarce biographical information is available about him.

MY CHILDREN

I anxiously polish my word with diamonds.
Who will understand it?
I anxiously turn my tears into fulgurating pearls.
What sight shall penetrate its brightness?

I am alone, night after night.
Night after night, I polish hearts.
I am wind and I am flame,
my word adheres to the palate:
pearls and diamonds burn in my lips . . .

I keep a handful of dark, brilliant accounts
in my expecting hand:
Who shall come?
Will anyone know they are but
particles of blood turn into pearls?

I spread diamonds through the seven chambers of hell;
crazed, I now fly, wind and night.
Street women,
left and right, have given birth to children,
and everywhere I have suffocated them
(still palpitating, tied to the nipple).

Ah my children, ah my children . . .

—Translated from Yiddish by Ilan Stavans

Carlos Grünberg

Carlos Grünberg (1903–1968) was an Argentine poet born in Buenos Aires. He was among the most important and influential of Jewish authors of his generation in Argentina. At the University of Buenos Aires, he earned advanced degrees in philosophy and law. In his early volumes of poetry, *Las cámaras del rey* (1922) and *El libro del tiempo* (1924), Grünberg showed a close affiliation with the group of 1920s avant-garde writers. His poetry collection *Mester de Judería* appeared in 1940. In the prologue Jorge Luis Borges stated that the book exemplified "the honor and pain of being Jewish in the incredible, perverse world of 1940." Carlos Grünberg was also known for his translations of Heinrich Heine and Chaim Nachman Bialik into Spanish. He was active in the Zionist movement and was named a liaison between the State of Israel and Argentina in 1948.

NEO-JEWS

Hello, Luxembourgers and Frenchmen
and Belgians and Dutchmen,
Danes and Norwegians,
Estonians, Latvians, Lithuanians, and Poles,
Austrians and Czechs and Slavs!
Oh, Yugoslavs, Albanians, Greeks!
Distant Indochinese!
Remote Filipinos!
Until recently we were we and you.
We the Jews and you the others.
We were the abject.
You were the select.
We the allogeneic and exotic,
the strange and eccentric.
We the autochthonous and indigenous,
aboriginal bodies and earthborn souls.
We, the expelled, the vile exiles.
You the earth tillers, firmly fixed and rooted.
We the wanderers.
You the inhabitants.
We without.
You with a state.
Now we are the dregs and throwaways
raised from below.
And now we are all Judaism.
The rising has left an abyss.
And now we are all—we and you—
Jews, one and another intensely Jewish,
eternally Jewish.
And newfangled Jewish,

permanently Jewish,
recently Jewish,
and currently Jewish,
perennially Jewish,
and up-to-date Jewish.
Jew with beards and beardless youths.
Old Jews and new Jews!

—Translated from Spanish by Stephen A. Sadow and J. Kates

HINTLER

As a result of the speech that the chance-
llor Hitler declaimed in the Reich-
stag on January 30, 1934, on the
occasion of the first anniversary of the
National Socialist regime and that
Was spread by radiotelephony
To the whole world.

The blood—y chan—cellor
expelled an anomaly
in the annipervers—ary
of his ferocious tyranny.

The homily of the Farted
Hatchet—man in Germany,
Spread from his back—side
By radiotelephony

The riffraff legion—s
From a certain beer hall
Heard his ser—mon.

And I quickly roared:
"Bravo for the *can—ary's* voice!"
And the rabble applauded me.

He applauded, the course one.
And I, happy, said to myself,
"*Jew dog*" Li—ar!

—Translated from Spanish by Stephen A. Sadow

César Tiempo

Born Israel Zeitlin in Ukraine, César Tiempo (1906–1980) was a poet, writer, playwright, screenwriter, and journalist who arrived in Buenos Aires as an infant and became a citizen in 1924. A member of the Boedo Writers Group, he also served as director of the Cervantes National Theatre between 1973 and 1975. Among his plays are *El teatro soy yo* (1933) and *Pan criollo* (1937). In his books of poetry—*Libro para la pausa del sábado* (1930), *Sabatión argentino* (1933), *Sábadodomingo* (1938), and *Sábado pleno* (1955)—Tiempo wrote sensitively and sometimes critically about the Jewish community of Buenos Aires. He was controversial for his defense of Peronism.

HARANGUE ON THE DEATH OF CHAIM NACHMAN BIALIK

How can a people who drag along
in their own darkness and their own depths
think about anything other than the here and now?

—BIALIK

On July 5th the Associated Press informed the world:
Chaim Nachman Bialik had died in Vienna.

And twenty days later in the same city
they shot Dollfuss, the "Millimetternich."

Watch out for poets
who pound their fists on the executioner's tables!

Community newspapers
managed to insert a note on the society page
next to the account of a party
thrown by the Barabanchiks
for the circumcision of an offshoot.

I have a violent heart
and a raspy voice.

I walk the crossroads in Jewish neighborhoods,
carrying rancor and pain on my back.

Brothers of Buenos Aires:
our greatest poet has died.
As in the Psalms

God girded his strength and perfected his way.
Minkowsky was the teardrop,
Bialik the imprecation.

And both rot under the earth,
facing the blind eyes of the terrifying night.

A sky in shirtsleeves runs over roof tiles.

Peddlers go on with day-night games of domi-
noes in cafes.

Girls who don't want to get married don't step under
ladders.

Middle-class gentlemen, you break all Ten
Commandments
and show up on the Sabbath with your black-
bound books,
touching them along their figured spines
to make them run off like cats.
I have seen you in the shining temples
—distinguished like bluebloods in luxurious
chains—
wearing high hats and *taleisim* of pure silk—
with a bribe for God,
who knows you better than your own employees,
Chaim Nachman Bialik has died.

Today in "The International" they serve stuffed fish
and a good stock of doctors for your poor languishing daughters.
Who remembers the Ukrainian massacres,
the feverish thunder of the pogroms,

when hooligans raped your mothers
and you huddled in cellars, afraid and helpless
like the light that licks mirrors?

Bialik cried out, thundered against the black waters,
and an angry laughter ran like a mad wind
through the hamlets.
"The people are like a withered grass,
and they are become like a dry stick."
And there were young men who learned to
rouse themselves like wolf cubs
and their sharp teeth lacerated our humiliation.

Chaim Nachman Bialik has died.

The junk dealers go on smiling in the seaports
of their pandemonium.

The Lacroze streetcars are as green as ever.

Cast your bread on the waters, Ecclesiastes says.

How enjoyable to hear Mischa Elman from a box in the Colón Opera
House.

Gorky said that with Bialik the Jewish people had given the world a
new Homer.

But how good is his credit at the Jewish Bank?

Voices:
—Tonight, when we close up, when I dunk

toast in a cup of tea, I'm going to ask my wife
to read me "To a Bird" and "My Garden," and
after we eat we're off to the Ombú Theater to
show how cultured we are.

Chaim Nachman Bialik has died.

—Mama, is it all right if I wash my hair with
kerosene and put on the light blue satin dress
and go to the library?—Fine, dear, maybe
you'll find a boyfriend, the way the other girls do.
It's about time.

Chaim Nachman Bialik has died.

At the entrance to the soup kitchen, our brothers, those who don't
dare die of
hunger, wait for their portion.

Chaim Nachman Bialik has died.

Our legs muck through the deepest waters of
nighttime, and over our head shines a pure
light.

In Tel Aviv there was a poet.

And now?

—Translated from Spanish by Stephen A. Sadow and J. Kates

Lázaro Liacho

Argentine poet, narrator, essayist, and journalist Lázaro Liacho (1906–1969), whose original name was Eliezer Liachovtzky, was born in Buenos Aires. He wrote articles for *Mundo Israelita* and *Judaica* but won recognition mainly as a poet. His books include *Bocado de pan* (1931), *Pan de Buenos Aires* (1940), and *El hombre y sus moradas* (1961), all of which reflect his outlook both as a Jew and as an Argentinean. His collection of stories *Sobre el filo de la vida* (1969) is about the Holocaust. Although he expressed admiration for Israel and Zionism, he considered Jewishness as a spiritual reality to be practiced anywhere and he praised Argentina as "the new Zion" in the poems included in *Siónidas desde la pampa* (1969). In his later work Liacho turned to biblical, religious, and metaphysical themes.

TO BE BORN JEWISH

To be born Jewish is a glory that comes dear.
Hard to carry on among the Christians.
It's bad to grow up Jewish among pagans,
their unreasoning reason is all too clear.

In the end, men bind us, keep us apart.
Good and evil tying brothers together.
We become the playthings of those blackguards
who turn what should be justice into a farce.

To be born Jewish is not, is not a gift.
No one chooses a future so dark.
No one wants to suffer so much affliction.

To be born Jewish is to weep in atonement,
to be a bird without a nest, migratory.
For being born Jewish there is no pardon.

—Translated from Spanish by Stephen A. Sadow and J. Kates

LOVE

If my desire to be Jewish is so great
that all the love I proclaim is true,
for love for the just, I hope for the good,
because I trust in the eternity of love.

Neither crying nor exile for being Jewish
will keep me from caring, loyally, wholly,
this exalted love, a form of God, bright star
of justice in which I trust.

In the uncontrollable world, sailor,
engulfed in the sea that batters Jewishness,
eager to prevent us from crossing.

Uncertain condition of defiance
on turbulent waves, one on watch,
seeing beaches of love in which I trust.

—Translated from Spanish by Stephen A. Sadow and J. Kates

Simón Zeleviansky

Simón Zeleviansky (1911–1979) emigrated with his Hasidic family from Minsk, Belarus, to Buenos Aires, where his mother and sister were killed during the Semana Trágica. Only a few poems of his survive. He was a peddler in Cartagena, Colombia, where he met his Iranian wife. In 1940 they immigrated to Caracas, Venezuela, where he worked first in a refugee agency for Holocaust survivors, then in the oil industry. Zeleviansky, his wife, and his daughter moved to Tehran, where they lived until the fall of Mohammad Reza Shah Pahlavi in 1978. He translated portions of *The Arabian Nights* from Farsi into Yiddish.

BY THE RIVER PLATE

I weep by the River Plate.

Beware, Argentina, of your false promises,
of the hatred you've inherited,
of your dreams of grandeur,
of the shop owner who believed in hard labor,
of the raped girl whose child is now yours,
of your abrupt patriotism,
and your exclusionary dreams.

If I forget who I am, let my right hand be cut off
and my tongue cling to my palate.

Beware of the ruins that inhabit you
and of those who want to witness your shame,
of the anger you've incubated,
of the newspaper boy who has lost an arm,
of your silent prophets,
of your negligent leaders,
and of your barren future.

If I forget who I am, let my right hand be cut off
and my tongue cling to my palate.

Remember, Argentina, the Semana Trágica:
"Rip him out," my attackers cried;
"send him back to where he belongs."
Now I'm a victim again,
spilling the same blood as in Kishinev,
witnessing the same atrocities as in Yekaterinoslav.

Why did you seek refuge in you?
I am Shylock once more—in spite of myself.

If I forget who I am, let my right hand be cut off
and my tongue cling to my palate.

Beware, Argentina, of populating your lands
with cadavers that cannot speak
and with the truth that won't relent.
Your heart is unyielding,
your soul a carcass,
your handshake a handcuff,
your morality upside down.

I weep by the River Plate.

—Translated from Yiddish by Ilan Stavans

Lucia Aizim

Born in Ukraine, Lucia Aizim (1915–2006) immigrated to Brazil with her mother and sister Luba in 1919. Little biographical information is available about her. She came to the city of Rio de Janeiro, where her parents already lived. She graduated from the Candido Mendes Commercial Academy, and then worked for a few years. Aizim also wrote a number of art songs. She married and became a homemaker.

WANDERING

I didn't know where that ship
would take us
slowly through the black sea. Certainly
I knew that the ship was not for pleasure.
For the grave faces, for the closeness of the bodies.
Something was telling me, a five year old,
that we were crossing the sea.
Even though it wasn't stormy. There was even moonlight
on some nights.

The ship was so sad,
so full of memories of those who were leaving.
And I still didn't know how to make things out. Between one city
and another. Everything was sea.
And unknown.
Only a few palm trees remained in my memory,
a few palm trees only.
Then those routes where we wouldn't stay
longer than for a short daybreak. Or from darkened port to port
involved in haze.
Little baggage, almost none.
We would go, frightened, for sure.

Where our heads would rest, at last?
Somehow, we still held onto some hope
of arriving, someday, at the chosen land.
And you were, among the americas
brasil
island profile
that welcomed us
with
your name of tree over all trees.

—Translated from Portuguese by Regina Igel

Julia Galimare

Born in Montevideo, Uruguay, of Sephardic Jewish parents, Julia Galemire (1923–) studied in the School for the Humanities at the University of the Republic of Uruguay. Deeply involved with the nation's culture, she was a member of the Association of Writers of Uruguay, acting as its undersecretary. In 1994 she founded the cultural group La Tertulia. She did cultural journalism for the CX 38 SODRE radio station in Montevideo, and for the program *La Tertulia,* which she has directed and coordinated for many years. In 1999 she was selected to edit the book *Letras de la paz,* a publication supported by UNESCO. Galimare has published ten books of poetry, among them the prize-winning *Fabular de la niebla* (1997), *La mujer y el ángel* (2000), and *Memoria silenciosa* (2013). In *Diario poético* (2005), Galimare reflects on her relationship with God.

POETIC DIARY I

I wish that the Great Computer
of earth, sea, and sky (as a
notoriously agnostic friend used
to call God) would teach me to think
and live in this world that
we understand less and less.
I know that if interminable
darkness should follow
I will know something of
the mystery our life implies.

—Translated from Spanish by Stephen A. Sadow and J. Kates

Humberto Costantini

Born in Buenos Aires of Italian Sephardic Jewish origin, Humberto Costantini (1924–1987) was a veterinarian by profession, but much of his life was engaged with literature and politics. He joined the Communist Party but later left the party when he became disenchanted with Stalin. He first published a book of short stories, *De aquí no más* (1958). His first collection of poems was *Cuestiones con la vida* (1966.) In 1973 he wrote *El libro de Trelew*, an epic tribute to his companions shot in that prison. *Cuestiones con la vida* (1974) was his next book of poems. *De dioses, hombrecitos y policías* (1979) is a novel written during the Argentine dictatorship as Costantini escaped to Mexico; it won Cuba's Casa de la Américas Award. While in Mexico, he wrote his political novel *La larga noche de Francisco Sanctis* (1984). He returned to Argentina in 1983. There he published his collected theater *Chau, Pericles* (1986). Throughout his turbulent life, Costantini wrote poetry on Jewish themes and championed Jewish values of social justice.

I POINT OUT

It's not that I'm lacking doubt or sadness,
nor that I find myself with a deficit of troubles,
nor that I'm poor in loneliness or anxieties,
nor that I have an everyday neurosis
where I fall down dead. No, nothing like that,
thank God.
I have my little account in the bank of aggravation
like any mortal.

It only happens that troubles are nauseating bugs,
loneliness spins you around like typhus,
breakups generally come
with shouting, doors, hatreds,
furious insults,
hands at your throat,
and sometimes with
a soft, silly, interminable cry like a child's,
begging for forgiveness.

Only sadness
is dirty, miserable, disturbing, and useless,
resisting the machine
and the pretty colors of twilight.
Only that it is neurosis
wanting me to tell you
it seems like idiocy.

—Translated from Spanish by Stephen A. Sadow and J. Kates

MY JOB

They ought to know
that when there is no work in the office, I work,
I break my ass,
I sweat ink,
I walk behind blue birds,
my dreams make trouble for me,
words bleed me dry,
I go out hunting whales and twilights,
I tame elephants
(you have to see how furious the jungle is),
I explain these times to the Pharaoh,
I occasionally make love,
I fight hand to hand with Zulus,
I have to make my way through perfume,
return by twelve o'clock,
die,
walk with my memories.

I have to speak with God,
go crazy, proclaim justice,
escape the stake,
never dress for a funeral.

I never rest even for a moment,
I raise a ruckus with the cicadas,
I meet with Lenin and repair the world,
I call long distance,
I say: Make a note in my agenda: Nazarene,
I try things in the air with the gulls,
I buy greens, blues, yellows

and I send them off by express into the sky.
I make an arrangement with clouds,
I sign off on autumn with a little rain,
I run to change faltering stars.
I promote honeysuckles, I dictate winters . . .
when my boss looks at me and says, ahem,
as long as you're not busy and have time.

—Translated from Spanish by Stephen A. Sadow and J. Kates

Arminda Ralesky

Arminda Ralesky (1924–2006) was born in Buenos Aires, a child of parents who came to Argentina from Ukraine. She was a teacher specializing in pre-school education and poetry, with studies in journalism and social psychology, as well as theatrical and cinematographic methodology. She obtained several awards for her literary work, including the prestigious, international Fernando Jeno Award in Mexico. Her work was very popular in Buenos Aires and often presented with musical accompaniment.

VI

My heart,
Pensive, fallible dreamer,
Meditates, sympathizes,
Thinks about its loved ones.

My mind loves.
Loves and understands the young,
Their anguish, pain, rebellions . . .
I follow, like my old ancestors,
Thinking with the heart
And loving with the head.
So Jewish, like my old Jewish ancestors.
In the obscure, profound origin
That never sees the clarity
And pushes the tree toward the light.

—Translated from Spanish by Stephen A. Sadow and J. Kates

Andrés Berger-Kiss

Andrés Berger-Kiss (1927–2016) was born in Hungary. His parents were actors who fled just before the Holocaust, in which fourteen members of his father's family perished. They arrived in Medellín, Colombia, in 1931. Berger-Kiss studied at the University of Antioquia in Medellín. He obtained a PhD in clinical psychology from the University of Missouri, was a clinical psychologist, and taught psychology in several universities. Later he became Director of Mental Health Education for the state of Oregon. Then he decided to dedicate his time exclusively to his writing. Andrés Berger-Kiss wrote more than thirty works of fiction and poetry, including his prize-winning story "The Sharpener." Berger-Kiss considered Colombia to be his second homeland. His poetry decries the Holocaust and exalts the Colombian countryside.

I DO NOT WANT THIS WOUND TO HEAL

For the Hungarian Swedish scientist George Klein,
the other one of the two of us who survived.

They say that time cures all evils,
And I would like to believe them.
But how will I be able to find relief
As one of the two survivors?

And I would like to believe them.
But how will I be able to find relief
As one of the two survivors,
Knowing that eight out of every ten of us
Were torn from our homes and murdered?

How will I be able to find relief?
I indulged myself while hunger swept away six million.
They say that time cures all evils,
But more than half a century has come and gone
Since eight out of ten of us
Were tortured while I was
Among the two that weren't even touched.

Not always, but often enough,
When I sit down at the table to share
A good and abundant meal,
I think about the times that went by,
Wishing I could put food in the mouths
Of the eight out of every ten
Whose lives were cut short.

Or taking my walk along the lovely embankment
Where the river turns beside my garden,
At times I can only think that
It takes no more time for me
to wake up than it took for the eight
to gasp for air in the chambers of Auschwitz.

Could I have forgotten them as I have many others?
If it were not for this deep wound
That I have carried with me for the greater part
Of my life? If it were so, even before
That natural death approaches,
How could I hope that the strangers,
Those who were informed at a distance, know and feel?

No! I do not want this wound to heal!

—Translated from by Stephen A. Sadow and J. Kates

Leonor Scliar-Cabral

Leonor Scliar-Cabral (1929–) holds a doctorate from the University of São Paulo and a postdoctoral degree from the University of Montréal. She is professor emerita at the Federal University of Santa Catarina. In 1991 she became president of the International Society of Applied Psycholinguistics and is currently an honorary member. She was president of the Brazilian Union of Writers (1995–1997) and was a finalist for the Jabuti Prize for her book *Sagração do Alfabeto* in 2010.

SHAVUOT IN GRANADA

Your small feet go up the alleys
through the Alhambra gardens and rose bushes,
awaiting the full moon.
Ripe pomegranates handed from your basket
and from the vineyards, bunches of grapes,
awaiting the full moon.
With the sweet-smelling orange blossom
you will adorn the stars,
awaiting the full moon.
And the bells sound their blessing
and Rabbi Yosef started reading,
awaiting the full moon.
Before the color of blood in the full moon
halts this wellspring forever
of an unfinished and eternal strength.

—Translated from Portuguese by Regina Igel

SEPHIROT

In a lost sphere a paradise
waits for me I don't know when
and I go on climbing in circles the branches
dry of fruits.
My gray hair is disheveled
a mask for dried out thorns,
where I searched for pomegranates, apples, and figs
from paradise.
I'm lost, but never my dream
and my torn cracked skin moans
for the last drops that feed
what is dead.

—Translated from the Portuguese by Regina Igel

Héctor Yánover

Born near Córdoba, Argentina, poet and bookseller Héctor Yánover (1929–2003) was a Virgil for Argentine literary references. He hosted the TV show *La librería en casa,* on which he counseled readers. His books include *Hacia principios del hombre* (1951), *Elegía y gloria* (1958), *Las iniciales de amo* (1960), and *Sigo andando* (1982) In 1973 he also published *Memorias de un librero* (Memories of a Bookseller), perhaps Yánover's most popular work. He was deeply concerned with the anti-Semitism he encountered in Buenos Aires.

NOW

Now I want to say I am Jewish
And I assume that identity even with
Its curse.
Now I want to reclaim all my brothers
From those who wrote the Bible to
Contemporary wretches.
Now I want to raise all the colors of my flag.
Because I have been all of them, even
The apostates.
Now I want to hate all those who hate me
Down through the ages and not pardon them.
Now I want to provide the way the king provides
And feel myself brother to my brothers and not be
The only one.
Now I want to cry for all the dead
And for all the injustices, and we offer to pay hatred
To the just.
I raise in my blood all blood.
I assume in my body all bodies,
I, the dead one.

—Translated from Spanish by Stephen A. Sadow

CAT, HELP THE POET

Cat, help the poet
Give him the dream of eating the rooster on the weather vane
Give him paths for his feet
And seven lives full of gorges and test tubes
So that he suffers to get the skills of living and knowing
Oh, cat without boots, don't abandon him
Meow at him from the corners, run him again
I want to see him rushed, going from one side to the other
Impatient and fantastic as I saw him yesterday
Cat, I ask of you, if you are a dream from along the way
Appear again
Give him wailing, panting, bristling at his senses
Make him believe.

—Translated from Spanish by Stephen A. Sadow and J. Kates

Juan Gelman

A poet and leftist political activist born in Buenos Aires, Juan Gelman (1930–2014) was exiled from his country in the 1970s. Gelman was jailed in the early 1960s during the Peronists' struggle for control of the federal government in Argentina. His political activism and his involvement with the Montoneros, a left-wing Peronist group that used violence in its efforts to overthrow the military government, resulted in his being forced into exile in Italy in 1975. He returned to Argentina briefly in 1988 before moving to Mexico. Gelman released his first collection of poetry, *Violín y otras cuestiones*, in 1956. Among his books of poetry are *El juego en que andamos* (1959), *Gotán*,(1962), *Interrupciones I* (1988), *Interrupciones II* (1988), *Salarios del impío* (1993), *Dibaxu* (1994), *Mundar* (2007), *El emperrado corazón amora* (2011), *Hoy* (2013), and *Amaramara* (2014). He taught himself Ladino to write *Dibaxu*. Gelman's Jewish heritage is present throughout his poetry.

END

Poetry isn't a bird.
And is.
It isn't a lung, air, my shirt,
no, nothing like that. And all of it.
Yes.
I have broken a violet against the sunset
to see what happened.
I went to the stone and asked what happened.
But no. But no.
Not yet.
Did I perhaps forget that handkerchief,
on which an old waltz circles in silence?
I didn't forget it, look at my cheek
and you'll see, no, I didn't forget it.
Did I forget the wooden horse?
Touch in me the child and you'll say no.
And so what?
Poetry is a way of living.
Look at the people at your side.
Do they eat? Suffer? Sing? Cry?

Help them fight for their hands, their eyes, their mouth, for the kiss to kiss and the kiss to give away, for their table, their bread, their letter *a* and their letter *h*, for their past—were they not children?—for their present, for the piece of peace, of history and happiness that belongs to them, for the piece of love, big, small, sad, joy, that belongs to them and is taken away in the name of what, of what?

Your life will then be an innumerable river to be called
pedro, juan, ana, maría, bird, lung, the air, my shirt, violin, sunset,
stone, that handkerchief, old waltz, wooden horse.
Poetry is this.
Afterward, write it.

—Translated from Spanish by Ilan Stavans

EPITAPH

A bird lived in me.
A flower traveled in my blood.
My heart was a violin.

I loved and didn't. But sometimes
was loved. I also
was happy: about the spring,
the hands together, what is happy.

I say a man has to be!

(Herein lies a bird.
A flower.
A violin.)

—Translated from Spanish by Ilan Stavans

DIBAXU: I

the tremor on my lips/
I mean: the tremor of my kisses
will be heard in your past
with me in your wine/

opening the door of time/
your dream
allows sleeping rain to fall/
give me your rain/

I will stop you/
still in your rain of sleep/
far inside the thinking/
without fear/ without forgetfulness/

in the house of time
is the past/
under your foot/
dancing

—Translated from Ladino by Ilan Stavans

Saúl Yurkievich

Saúl Yurkievich (1931–2005) was an Argentine poet and literary critic born in a Jewish immigrant family in La Plata, Argentina. In the 1950s he joined the avant-garde movement in Buenos Aires. Yurkievich began as a scholar and critic of Latin American literature, and his first published work, *Valoración de Vallejo* (1958), showed him to be a rigorous one. Yurkievich published his first poetry collection, *Volanda linde,* in 1961. In 1968 he moved to Paris, where he was a professor of Latin American literature at Paris 8 University Vincennes-Saint-Denis and lived for the rest of his life. He maintained a strong friendship and literary ties with Julio Cortázar. Yurkievich authored a remarkable poetic production rooted in the experimentalism of the 1960s. In his short stories and early poetry, he showed a profound knowledge of the Kabbalah and the uncanny aspects of Jewish life.

TUMBLES AND RUMBLES

so many accounts I count up
of all my losses
and all my muddles
subtracting and adding
as if the past
in addition to increasing
were able to correct
as if my present were
a matter of calculation
as if my future
would let itself be proved
there are abracadabras that work
no master keys
no precision instruments
for this flux
that zigzags
who knows how far and how long
that keeps cutting capers
on the trapeze

stop your tumbles and rumbles
little acrobat
you've already played clown and lion tamer
spotlights illuminate
the top of the tent
drums roll
here comes the somersault
be careful
don't fall

—Translated from Spanish by Cola Franzen

Raúl Hecht

Raúl Hecht (1931–2012) was born in Artigas, a small city in the north of Uruguay. He studied law and diplomacy in Montevideo and at the same time coordinated the Recital of New Poetry in the Teatro del Pueblo. He taught courses on the history of international treaties. In 1955 Hecht published *Amor constante*, his first poetry collection. In 1966 he returned to Artigas, where he engaged in crop and livestock agriculture and served as the director of the Agriculture Association. Over the years Hecht traveled regularly to Israel to visit his daughter, who had immigrated there. He wrote short stories and the poetry collection *Exodos y arraigos: Obra poética* (2000), in which he combines simple and sophisticated poems. Hecht was known as "The Poet of Artigas."

WHEN YOU OPEN THE WINDOW

For Dinorah in Israel

When you open the window
every morning,
think, daughter,
that you open yourself to the sun
to receive the day,
the sweet aroma
of the fruit trees,
the song of the pines
and the wind.

When you open the window
every morning,
feel, daughter,
that your eyes fill
with the ancestral hills,
in the land you have chosen
for the return.

When you look at the gaze
of your beloved,
how he looks at the sky
before the harvest,
or when the fruit is born,
smile, my daughter,
make your soul feel joy,
since, like Shabbat,
you are the bride
of the days.

When you open your window,
once
among so many,
and there are clouds in the sky
and nostalgia on your shoulders,
join your hands, daughter,
and leave a space in them;
you will then touch,
you will feel
a warm bird
beating,
living like a memory,
caressing
in time;

you will touch, daughter,
you will feel our heart
beating,
living like a memory
caressed in time;

you will touch, daughter,
you will feel our heart
beating,
warm bird
that has followed its flight
every day,
in all the days of your life,
singing your smile,
opening your wings
to cover the nest,
taking flight

to let yourself fly,
like the sun,
like the air
of every morning;
then you will smile,
and you will be happy,
since like Shabbat,
you are the bride of the days.

And you will be blessed
always,
my daughter,
in all the days of your life

—Translated from Spanish by Stephen A. Sadow and J. Kates

Marcos Silber

Marcos Silber (1934–2021) published eighteen books and participated in national and foreign anthologies. He was invited to the International Poetry Festivals in Medellín and Bogotá, Colombia; Cajamarca, Peru; and Caracas, Venezuela. He received the Sash of Honor from the Argentine Writers Society in 1968. He also obtained the Municipal Poetry Prize of the City of Buenos Aires, 1998-1999. He was a member of the Society of Living Poets and an honorary member of the Argentine Writers Society. Silber played an active role in the Jewish community and often turned to Jewish themes in his poetry.

I SEE HIM – 1911

I see him.
From the railing of the poem, I see him.
He's fourteen, he who will be my father.
He's coming on the *Arlanza*. He doesn't see me.
The land that waits for him has no face.
The ship that bites into waters of strange languages keeps coming on.
He who will be my father can't read or write.
Stock still, he carries the drawing of the letter.
I hear the shipwreck of his internal steam,
and his silence clubs me on the head.
Enormous darkness dances around him.
He is stung by the cold on deck.
The boy doesn't see me, but he teaches me:
"Anguish," make note of the word "anguish," son,
make note of "fright," and don't miss nothing "solitude."
A woolen word flies toward his neck,
another of protection falls across his shoulders.
He who will be my father can't read or write.
He breathes a green air of consolation.
When, in his happiest dream,
he dreams of me writing.
And he lays down his inescapable burden of labor
to teach me: Make note, son,
of the word "work" and "roof" and "bed"; make note
also of "chicken soup
with its floating gold coins."
I see him. He doesn't see me.
I hear him: "Take my hand, son,
guide it.
Let's write."

—Translated from Spanish by Stephen A. Sadow and J. Kates

Rosita Kalina

Rosita Kalina (1934–2004) was born in San José, Costa Rica. She graduated from the University of Costa Rica with a degree in English literature. She taught English at the high school level and helped to found the Santa Ana High School in San José. From 1965 to 1970 she lived in the United States. She then returned to the University of Costa Rica, where she taught English. Kalina published much short fiction in the literary supplements of *La Nación* newspaper in San José, for which she also wrote social criticism. She often contributed to *Herencia judía,* a Jewish journal in Bogotá, Colombia. In 1988 she was awarded the National Poetry Prize for her *Los signos y los tiempos.* Though not an observant Jew, in her poetry she frequently explored Jewish religious and existential themes in highly original poetry collections such as *Detrás de las palabras* (1983), *Cruce de niebla* (1987), *Mi paz guerrero* (1998), and *Los signos y los tiempos* (1987, 1999).

I AM OF THE TRIBE OF JUDAH

I am of the tribe of Judah.
That of my grandparents and great-grandparents.
That of Solomon, of Jesus and Einstein.
Not to mention Freud
whose valuable Kabbalistic secret
leaped to the therapist's chair.
I don't forgive the thousands of Holocausts
that in the name of false truths
were devised against my people,
against other extremely old peoples
wiser than the law of the powerful.
I am horrified by the man who takes part in religious wars.
That we are one in the immense ship
Mother Earth that transports to
unlimited dimensions.
That we all breathe like destiny.
I am universal. Simply a woman
who dares to dream of a brotherhood
of souls and of wings.
Precisely because of my origin,
I well understand the sadness of others
brought down by color or angle of eyes.
Let the era of man come,
marvelous being who populates existence!
In him I see as unique, unrepeatable
my pride of being a woman.
I also love the animal and the plants
that live my solitudes.
I am Jewish. Smooth even to the caress.
Loving even to ecstasy.

—Translated from Spanish by Stephen A. Sadow and J. Kates

TO TRANSCEND LIFE

I am learning to transcend life.
I am not frightened
by predatory eagles,
or tigers with exhausted eyes
that injure my solitary, flourishing brow.
Luminous openings,
fully ample,
sweetly sacred,
vibrate at my step.
I will arrive with serene maturity
to the mountains.
My candles will blow
with green winds
when the rainbow crosses through
the fog.
I wish for all
a lively awakening
of crystalline desires,
doves collecting from my palm
innocent grains.
We are made of a little of the phoenix
and a great deal of bonfires.
Perpetual spiral toward the summit,
sailors' waves,
hoving from the mud toward the blood.
Although at times we go in reverse.
Let's go up, travelers.

—Translated from Spanish by Stephen A. Sadow and J. Kates

Eliahu Toker

Eliahu Toker (1934–2010) wrote eight books of poetry, including *Lejaim* (1974) and *Padretierra* (1977). A prolific translator of poetry from Yiddish into Spanish, he has published *El resplandor de la palabra judía* (1981), an anthology of seventy Yiddish poets and more than three hundred poems. He also translated Hebrew classical texts, such as "El Cantar de los Cantares" (Song of Songs) (1984) and the Talmudic "Pirké Avot" (1988). He edited anthologies of Argentine Jewish writers, among these *Buenos Aires esquina: Sábado, vida y obra de César Tiempo* (1997). Toker was awarded the Sash of Honor by the Argentine Writers Society in 1982, 1989, and 1997. The Mexican Jewish community conferred upon him the Fernando Jeno Prize.

HOMAGE TO MY JEWISH CONDITION

My son is in no way like me,
as much as I am my father and precisely
the other side of the coin,
a same dune differently
modeled by storms.

So I don't let my history down.
I meticulously set the usual trap,
and under protest I place my hand inside,
sick and tired of my Jewish condition.

Reflected by myths that interweave tragedy,
my People is an inverted polyhedron
with convex panes of glass that move away from the doors
and the tic of repeating the misfortune, the fate.

My son is in no way like me,
as much as I am my father and precisely
the other side of the coin,
a same dune differently
modeled by storms.

—Translated from Spanish by Stephen A. Sadow and J. Kates

Sara Riwka B'raz Erlich

Psychiatrist, psychoanalyst, and writer Sara Riwka B'raz Erlich (1935–2013) was born in Recife, Pernambuco. She was the daughter of Polish Jews who arrived in Brazil before the Second World War. Erlich, who for a while lived in Israel, published scientific research and literary works in Brazil, England, Argentina, Israel, and Holland. Her books include *Histórias que precisavam ser contadas* (1965), *No tempo das acácias* (1978), and *No tempo das acácias e outros tempos* (2003), which deals with her experiences as a diaspora Jew and interweaves Brazilian culture with Eastern European and Jewish themes.

DAUGHTERS OF THE DIASPORA

To all the sisters of the Diaspora
of all places and times

Daughters of the Diaspora,
Transoceanic
in transit between worlds,
languages, cultures, rhythms, and strange things,
colors, sounds, smells, endearments, multiple expressions,
Acculturated.
Oceans, rivers, wild mangroves.
Transcultural inhabitants
wearing flowers and fruit of colors never seen before,
savored, paradisiacal,
more dreamlike than real.
Amaryllis . . .
Ice and fire.
Unique diaspora and interlaced with others,
sisters.
Roots violently torn out mutually supporting each other,
sewing themselves together.
Living tessitura, close-knit.
Blood, bones, viscera.
Cosmic ties.
Pain of the soul transfigured in Joy.
Far beyond the limited power of the Oppressor.

—Translated from Portuguese by Regina Igel

TRANSAZURE

Tranaz Traveler,
Man/Woman/Living Stones.
Hypnagogic Itinerary,
transitory,
transazure,
heralded.
Fatal Intersection.
Leaden tunic . . .
Green Light.
Entrapping smile of destiny.
Wings of the Shekinah.
Omen.
Eyes of a rare desert color.
Ripe dates.
Transcapibariberiver.
Timeless tears.
Lapis Lazuli.
Tunnel of transition.
Grand Passage.
Man's Crossing.
Serene, beautiful.
Pure, enchanted.
Splendor.
White Landscape.
Synthesis of all Landscapes.
Life and Death.
Transition.
Pulsations . . .
Solitude.
Woman risen

from the drops of lapis lazuli,
bathed in brilliance.
Vital tears.
Immemorial,
the core of golden Acacia petals
envelopes her like slumbering balm.
Psychic suffering, suffering of the soul, at last,
Transmuted into dream,
Reverie,
essence of Creation.
Unhinged.
Dying Passion.
Fragmented energy.
Love absorbed by Nature.
Vital Rhythm.
Renewal.
Magnetized Royal Eagle.
Ruddy Farewell.
Bloody,
reunion
possible
impossible.
Hope.
Longing.
Halleluyah!!!
Decline and Return
The Hour of Havdalah!

—Translated from Portuguese by Regina Igel

Angelina Muñiz-Huberman

Born in France and the daughter of Republican refugees from the Spanish Civil War, Angelina Muñiz-Huberman (1936–) lives in Mexico City. She traces her ancestry on her mother's side to converted Jews who never left Spain. After reading the Old Testament, its commentaries, and the mystical books of the Kabbalah, she formally converted to Judaism. Muñiz-Huberman was a professor of comparative literature at the Autonomous University of Mexico. She is the author of the novels *Dulcinea encantada* (1993), *El mercader de Tudela* (1999), and *El sefardí romántico: La azarosa vida de Mateo Alemán II* (2005). She is also the writer of many books of poetry, among them *El ojo de la creación* (1992), *La sal en el rostro* (1998), and *Rompeolas: Poesía reunida* (2012). Her favorite themes are creation and destruction and exile as a state of being. Muñiz-Huberman inserts her profound knowledge of Jewish mysticism into her poems.

THE KABBALISTS

From on high they received the divine voice,
the spark that kindles the heart.
They interpreted the word only from mouth to ear.
Nothing was kept in writing.
On water or on the river, yes.
With the nine attributes of the unnamable
added to the boundless sphere,
they sketched the tree of wisdom.
The scale of light,
the setting in exegesis.
Black fire in white fire.
The page does not say what it says
but says far more than it says.
Stopped on the shore of the lake,
high reeds all along the bank,
they throw a stone to a point equidistant
and concentric circles
expand, purifying the paths of knowledge.
Each one absorbs the lore that cautiously burnishes
between cut diamonds
for the novice who desires to refine
his sound and memory
and the dream of all things.

—Translated from Spanish by Stephen A. Sadow and J. Kates

THE EYE OF CREATION

in memory of Marcela Huberman

In the same way the white ibis runs
over grass that does not feel its weight
and three drops of blood redden its plumage
of soft curves
—three unperceived drops of blood—
and the brackish odor of fish-tainted water
blends with the odor of millenarian semen
In the same way the shadow runs to meet
the forgotten body
and doubles back into the hidden part of the fragile terrain
In the same way air labors among the lost
channels of windswept dunes
In the same way the final hour tolls
—although the dead man may not hear it—
and the distilled droplet of love rings
—although it may not surge underground—
it runs, doubles back, labors and tolls
the hidden river of quiet waters
of the eye of creation.

—Translated from Spanish by Stephen A. Sadow and J. Kates

THE PALACE AND SEPHARAD

The palace was born in Sepharad, at the edge of the river
so long and wide the eye could not embrace it;
towers touched the heavens, clouds withdrew.
Not everyone saw it, yet its song and the rhythm of its poetry were
heard.

Those departed into exile took it in their memory,
caring for it, polishing it, purifying it, chanting.

Each day, the palace reached high into dreams of return,
its walls crying, becoming nectar for the lonesome.

On winter nights, the palace held snow crystals,
which next morning became the well of trimmed desires.

In summer, swallows recognized in it their abandoned nests,
and fresh straw, dispersed feathers, wisps, and flakes of cotton
again embellished the forsaken palace's railings.

If someone came near, a curtain was drawn, and the palace disappeared.

No more intruders. Only the true owners lamented
lights in the interstices created rainbows in all colors.

Pilgrims capable of entering slept in beds of plumage,
waking at dawn before the hour of morning prayer.

They again set out on the voyage without stopping, hand to hand,
consecrating wine, their recently polished words becoming whole-
some chants.

For centuries of wait, the uninhabited palace kept standing.
It knew.
Sooner or later, the exiled were meant to return.

—Translated from Spanish by Ilan Stavans,
with Angelina Muñiz-Huberman and Alberto Huberman

PASSOVER

Immersed in memory, I lost myself in a light.
What star it came from, I could not say.

I opened the window and the scent of air
Climbed, like a moth, over the walls.

The lit candles were blown out,
And the spilt wine covered the tablecloth.

The moon shone on the white linen,
Illuminating the night of love.

One crossed the sea and all followed,
Awaiting an immense desert of liberty.

Stone and sand marked the way,
Songs and a dance of veils, and eternity.

Children framed their memory
With four questions only once engraved.

At midnight the owl spread its wings,
And the half-opened door became a blessing.

Travelers of all lands,
May you rest at last.

—Translated from Spanish by Ilan Stavans

Alejandra Pizarnik

Alejandra Pizarnik (1936–1972) was born into a family of Russian Jewish immigrants in Argentina. After studying philosophy and journalism (though she never earned a degree), Pizarnik began her artistic training with the surrealist painter Juan Batlle Planas. Between 1960 and 1964 she lived in Paris, where she worked for the magazine *Cuadernos* and studied at Sorbonne University. She was awarded the prestigious Guggenheim (1968) and Fulbright (1971) Fellowships, although she never completed her studies. Her works include *Inocencia* (1956), *Árbol de Diana* (1962), *Los trabajos y las noches* (1965), and *Infierno musical* (1971). Her works such as *Texto de sombra* and *Últimas poems* (1982) were published posthumously. Alejandra Pizarnik suffered a series of depressive crises that led her to attempt suicide. She was then admitted to a Buenos Aires psychiatric center. In 1972 she ended her life with an overdose of Seconal. She was thirty-nine years old.

POEM FOR THE FATHER

And it was then
that with a tongue dead and cold in the mouth
he sang the song others allowed him to sing
in this world of obscene gardens and shadows
coming at unseemly hours to remind him
of songs of his youth
in which he could not sing the song he wanted
the song they allowed him to sing
yet through his absent blue eyes
through his absent mouth
through his absent voice.
Then from absence's tallest tower
his song resonated in the opacity of what is hidden
in the silenced extension
full of moving hollowness like the words I write.

—Translated from Spanish by Ilan Stavans

ONLY

I finally understand the truth

it explodes in my desires

and in my miseries
in my disagreements
in my unbalances
in my delirium

I finally understand the truth

now
let's look for life

—Translated from Spanish by Ilan Stavans

Miryam Gover de Nasatsky

Miryam Gover de Nasatsky (1937–) was born in Buenos Aires and graduated with a degree in education from the National University of the Littoral. She edited the *Bibliografía de Alberto Gerchunoff* (1976). With Ana Weinstein she published *Escritores judeo-argentinos: Bibliografía 1900–1987* (1994). With Ana Weinstein and Roberto Nasatsky she also produced *Trayectorias musicales judeo-argentinas* (1998). Gover de Nasatsky wrote the fictionalized biographies *La pasión de un visionario: Theodor Herzl* (2004) and *Desde la cima: Reminiscencias de David Ben-Gurión* (2008), as well as the novel *Hacia la libertad* (2015) about the French Resistance during the Second World War. Her first book of poems, *Persistentes vibraciones*, appeared in 1999. The second, *Resonancias de Auschwitz* (2011), was inspired by a visit to the Auschwitz Museum.

GUARD TOWER

The sharp wail of a siren
pierced the silent barracks,
and shoes of all sizes,
in their hundreds or thousands,
lined up alone
in the prison yard,
endlessly mustered,
just as it is,
in a cold sweat of fear.
Terribly worn,
indefinitely colored,
but holding together
as if they might yet cover
the damaged feet
of those compelled to die
because they were Jews.
The smallest
still damp
with tears and urine
next to the remains of large
broken soles.
Silence and shock in the cold morning!
Stones, bricks, and barbs!
Another wail tried
to set them walking—in vain.
They are capable only of clustering together
until they are stacked
into
a sorrowful mountain.

Guard tower of shame,
they endure,
entrenched
without consolation
in the face of horror and impotence.

—Translated from Spanish by Stephen A. Sadow and J. Kates

Luisa Futoransky

Born in Buenos Aires, Luisa Futoransky (1939–) received her law degree in 1967. She attended the University of Iowa's International Writing Program, then worked as a journalist in Beijing and Tokyo before finally settling in France. Futoransky brings together cultural references inspired by her experiences of life in Latin America, Europe, and the Far East, which she mixes with distinctive images from Argentina. Her books include *Babel, Babel* (1968), *El diván de la puerta dorada* (1984), *Cortezas y fulgores* (1997), *Ortigas* (2014), and *Humus, humus* (2020).

JERUSA OF MY LOVE

in jerusa the days are long and since dawn, the people, such as they
are,
want to meddle—and they do so—inside the action movie

the cowboys of the Middle East spit out sunflower seeds, to which
further away
in the garden, one can stumble upon hedgehogs and porcupines
and in your own bed, scorpions, so is the land . . .
but on top of that, it occurred to allen to disappear during the Spring,
one afternoon
jerusa limit ana
allen, who left without convincing himself or convincing us
of what his mother, naomi, who loves him,
had been certain

while
everyone shouts
when they don't howl, included, in the privileged seating, the stones.

the storks hurry to leave and confuse the shipments,
virgins and celibate monks, anchorites, and guardians of the temples
pay the piper; are discounted because of us, the rest, also,
us, the payers of tithes, broken plates, the givers of blood,
bones and brains
among car horns, real alarms and not so much, imperative door-ringing
and empty telephones
wildflowers prosper, and I struggle tooth and nail, with ferocious
blows
to scratch the scabies like Marat's, among these/those charlotte cor-
day, zealots, essenes, illuminists,

all of them armed, except with patience

how many ays! jerusa of my love

today toward early morning, I saw it quickly run some embarrassed
drops
that hide brilliant desert poppies among those depending
on the thirsty tail,
milky, of the Hale-Bopp comet
that preaches, stubborn,
millennial nonsense.

at nightfall in the hotel among disjointed thorns from suppers and literary toasts, a healthy-looking and optimistic gentleman appears who says that I ought to recognize him as a member of my family, and he tells me that I should include, on his request, in my next novel, that one of my cousins run naked through the streets of rehovot, and when they find him, he says: "let's go to mama's," and they repeat to him that mama died long ago, like decades and more decades in remote buenos aires, and he begins to sigh: "don't tell me, don't tell me," and he lets himself be led, sweetly and wearily, home, and tomorrow he begins again to want to visit papa, and he remained in an irreversible way in some neighborhood, undressed, immune to the levantine winds, playing visits with those of the mist

the gentleman is named meir and insists in relating to me sagas from home and of everyday life: that cousin's little girl, whom they called queen esther for being beautiful and capricious, bought a pizzeria with the one who was then her almost husband, and just before the wedding she ditched him, but she kept the business and with us paying the mortgage; as a social worker the prisons were estercita's territory, and she ended up falling in love with her favorite prisoner, a boy who was a re-offender from the drug world but very good looking, no reason to deny it, and when he was freed conditionally one afternoon, some tough came to visit him, and nothing more was known of him, and ester was seen in two-column photos in the country's newspapers, fighting so that the rabbinate would declare her a widow because the body of the good-looking fellow never appeared and she, pregnant for eight months, wanted to marry a bookkeeper and settle down until even the rabbis said that they agreed but that she should not return to her wild ways and she is a legal widow and she left, meir said, on her way.

in the manuscripts of the dead sea the sons of light and the sons of darkness are in combat

to the renewed amazement of the studious and the rest of living
people, nobody has a name, nobody knows nor can differentiate
one from the other
it seemed those of the light won that by a hair
in order to convert themselves, it's well known, from the shadow of
what we were, are, and you will be.

I walk with my friend, the poet rami, chewing two hundred grams of shiny etrogs, we thresh certain healthy slander about absent colleagues, we interchange avatars of lovers, and occasionally, in puffs, we get drunk over the secret of the scribes of qitmit and of qumram, whose words can be read by children in school today, but the reality, the breath, backward and forward, not above and below

ay! jerusa of my heart, that of jesus and of jerusa, that of violent anemones and old men who ramble pained by incoherence in the very sunny nursing home my recent fascination, a poet with a name of purple and dark dahlias, who loses, by puffs, her reason, who finds his Cartier sunglasses, that likes so much to say that it's necessary to revise Genesis, she is sure that abraham our patriarch loved ismael more than isaac and for that reason didn't sacrifice him, of the women, not even she speaks, except of her mother whom she reveres as a legendary teacher because she taught her that the Jewish people for being singular and special has the obligation, the greatest, to be compassionate and I contemplate with shock the havoc that so much bloody idol, so many thorns, so much shrapnel causes the earth, the plants and the people

and what to say about the concept of "chosen"
source which waters all the craziest ideas
the injustices, the rigidities
the squares, the wells
the poisoned checkerboards, the griefs without consolation,
Dahlia, I move away from you, I feel sorry for you, softly
and I shake my handkerchief in goodbye
to belong to the sect described in the rolls
it was necessary to have nine evident exterior characteristics
like being pallid in sunny lands, long fingers, a non-rosy complexion
and more, much more
with six qualities, the adept is tested for two years and, on being
well judged, he passes to novice, a servant
of whom, of whose.
ah! the cunning scholars of qitmit . . .

proud, magnanimous, the fleshy plants of aloe vera
could calm down the burns of this zoo and what's left of the solar
system
the energy of those who come hopes for

just a minimum of trust
this is, the salem, the cardamon, the rosemary, the pepper
the sex of life

here the adventurers come by heavy seas that later we catalog
somberly in alphabetical order
what/how/who
with *s* they were, for example, the cutlases, the scimitars of saladin
and suleiman,
the minarets, armories, the victories that rot into defeats
a synthetic hodgepodge, animist and syncretic at both sides of the
principal route of
rusts of the 48, the 67, the day of fasting and pardon

to plant in the desert, it is necessary to wash the earth without ceasing
because the sea at arm's reach is called death or
makes it seem that way
so that the situation is the same

in Spring the national flower is humble and wild, of a brilliant red,
leaves behind a brief and blazing trickle that drives to despair the
cardinal points
of heavenly Jerusalem and splashes, gives off sparks of outrage on the
terrestrial

I attend the court of peace, what an obsessive reiteration with the end an audience where my brother defends, his trade, a young man who appears shackled by hands and feet before the judge of having extorted with a knife at the other's jugular 100 shekels from a pious and religious citizen to provide himself a dose of what in Hebrew is called manna; as he knew that 80 would be enough for him, he returned 20 to the individual who later recognized him and reported him. I keep

forever his in my left pocket near my heart his crafty and beaten
pocket knife, and I also say goodbye to him
goodbye

these sediments of guffaws and killings look at me
of exemplary taciturnity
I make my way through unruly meows
giant and twisted geraniums
I fill myself up with intimate and street fritters
of tiles
and I pretend that I leave

then I receive by voice, an indispensable
tangled obituary
that I hang to my neck prepared
with dark pearls from ancient tears:
I want you to know that mama, I love you.
Sonia

Tivon, Israel, April 14, 1997

—Translated from Spanish by Stephen A. Sadow

David Turkeltaub

Born in Santiago, Chile, David Turkeltaub (1936–2008) worked as a copyeditor and in various other jobs. He traveled to Brussels, Madrid, and Guatemala. During the military dictatorship he was director of the *Editorial Ganymides*, a beautiful magazine and one of the few periodicals at the time that published Nicanor Para, Enrique Lihn, Gonzalo Rojas, and José Donoso. His poetry volumes are *Hombrecito verde* (1979), *Códices* (1981), and *Los arrepentimientos* (1984), which includes "Geratevet."

GERATEVET

Geratevet is a word that I heard often when I was a child.
Samuel was saved from Treblinka,
Sonia was saved from Dachau.
Moisés, Raquel were not able to be saved,
or: we don't know if they were saved.
Er ot sich geratevet is a phrase that I heard often when I was a child
though in the majority of times I heard it as a question:
was he saved?
That was after the badges.
My father kept the atlas and the badges
and began asking who had been saved.
My infancy, then, is a pricked map
and the word *geratevet.*

—Translated from Spanish by Stephen A. Sadow

Aída Gelbtrunk

Born in Montevideo, Uruguay, Aída Gelbtrunk (1939–1999) was a distinguished and popular Uruguayan poet, novelist, and film critic. She was also an influential member of the Uruguayan Jewish community. Her collections of poetry, among them *Causa des sí* (1987), deal with deep emotions and issues of hope and despair, at times mystically. She was an early writer of magical realism. Her novel *Aire de familia* (1998) is based on Jewish life in Uruguay before and during the 1940s. Aída Gelbtrunk died suddenly in New York City.

YOU ALREADY FEEL THE AIR BEARING RAIN

You already feel the air bearing rain. Mama entered the kitchen. The
cadavers of the roses were on the table, with petals of paper and
living beings, full of sap, of blood. And they were living
ones and dead ones, like children. She took a branch of
parsley and cut it, and stars sprouted among its leaves.
Her hands were salty; from the ceiling pearl after pearl and
butterflies with only one wing, a pheasant with blue feathers and a
gold beak, full of soul, began to appear.
She didn't speak, only looked. She hears herself like the
sound of rain, of silver, of gold.
Why are you so solitary, Aída?
She looked at me with her nostalgia, secret tendency, with
all her memory.
The pictures on the walls spoke and smiled and returned to
being serious. Until the stars, full of stars, were discovered to hang
from the sky, flickering and conspiring.

—Translated from Spanish by Stephen A. Sadow

ALL ILLUSION IS A FORM OF HOPE

and faith knows nothing of reasons.
In some hidden tracing of Scripture
you can find human destiny, the luminous sphere, the womb,
the wound of error and the early scent of
redemption.
God with man, man with his god,
like one half with its half of light
attempting, tasting, barely touching,
to be
in actual existence:
to feel
with minute pleasure
the stubborn celestial light
that becomes an erect cry,
that seeks the exit from its body
to create
in a unique present,
in a free act of love,
    —in its error, its fear and marvel—
with the intimate perplexed fruits,
in work released from nothingness
like a blank sheet of paper
that waits to be dug out from within
in a new form,
filling the flights by fits and starts.

—Translated from Spanish by Roberta Gordenstein

José Kozer

Born in Havana, Cuba, of Jewish parents who had emigrated from Poland and Czechoslovakia, José Kozer (1940–) left Cuba in 1960 and lived in New York City until 1997, when he retired from his position as full professor at Queens College after teaching Spanish and Latin American literature for thirty-two years. After living for two years in Spain, he then moved to Florida. His poetry has been translated into many languages, has been widely anthologized, and has appeared in many literary journals around the world. His prolific body of work now includes 14,150 poems and more than 103 books of poetry that have been translated into multiple languages. He is the recipient of the Pablo Neruda Ibero-American Poetry Prize, the Montgomery Fellowship, and the City University of New York's Gertrudis Gómez de Avellaneda Prize.

PASSOVER IN HAVANA

This is the day of Passover.
This is the day Jews recline
over the day-to-day buying and selling,
passing through Beirut, landing in Havana,
this is the day they set up a synagogue, open a Cuban grocery,
and gather in all the offspring from the diaspora.
It's just the time that Daniel Santos tips it off, kicks it off, led by the
    Casino Band,
Jacobo gives Maria Brull a box of perfumed soaps,
Toña la Negra breaks loose a beat boxed in on TV,
the Jews confirm the act of the alliance.
The Jews retreat within themselves to grieve the absence of water.
They shrivel up, miserably clutching the four legs of the votive table,
chewing the bread of the offering over the four corners of the earth,
lamenting the merciless exile of prohibitions,
attentively listening to Aaron's forefathers and Elohim,
the wrath of the mount that makes us rich and makes us want
an eye for an eye, a tooth for a tooth,
day by day, the Jews confirm the prodigious atonement of the Sons
of Israel,
made to pay fivefold steer by steer,
crop for crop, ox for ox,
father for father, irremediably repaying the law of the Decalogue.

—Translated from Spanish by Stephen A. Sadow and J. Kates

DIASPORA

The store in Havana is dust,
the white Irish fabric ground to dust,
and my father, a crumpled-up Jew,
comes back day after day with a loaf of rye under his arm.
He comes back day after day, always the same,
his eyes slanted from the twill pinstripes,
unlike a skipper darting his eyes.
Coming home he seems a light and jagged crater.
Father comes and we eat staring at the molding around the ceiling.
I never saw water. I don't see a fish or a plant.
My mother polishes the edges of the furniture again. She changes
Thursday sheets.
We don't see a flower in any of the bedrooms.
All the stores in Havana have been shut,
the workers zealously taken to the streets,
and my father, a crumpled-up Jew,
bears the Ark of the Law again on leaving Cuba.

—Translated from Spanish by Stephen A. Sadow and J. Kates

Juana Ciesler

Argentine poet Juana Ciesler (1941–2014) studied literature at the University of Buenos Aires and music at the Manuel de Falla Municipal Conservatory. During that period she began publishing her books of poetry: *De ufos y veredas* (1966), *El fuego en los palacios de agua* (1969), *La misión de las máscaras* (1982), *Tulipanes en la cabeza* (1986), *Celeste y negra* (1989), *Los sueños del ADN* (1999), *Canción de la tierra* (2001), and *La sexta década* (2006). Her poems appear in many anthologies of Argentine literature. Ciesler's poetry mixes past and present, melancholy and hope.

HIS BROTHER ZALMAN

Either Buma or Sasha who loved this poem

He could not have dreamed it.
For the first time, thirty-four years had gone by,
he turned "to see" his brother Zalman,
receptacle of ghosts or nocturnal visitors,
in the play of a man acting inside a few three centimeters of cerebrum
underlying the theorem of dimensions.
He could never have emerged from his
homeland tomb earth.
The story awarded him death
in a fusillade at the edge of the forest
on the last day of the war, not
before "hearing" the last cry of each one
of his three children, of her who had given him the children.
The brother returned in a dusk of chestnuts.
"I have been waiting for you a long time. You are late."
The heaviness of the hand on his shoulder
covered by the absence of a white shroud
when the handsome athlete might have married the orphaned
sister of the only brother in far-off lands.
The East, no.
America, no.
The last remaining brothers in the far-off Polish land,
once Lithuanian, another time Bolshevik,
turn their backs on an ochre dawn, go away
far along the path.
The aged grandmother, young guest of the odorless waves

of the bloodied shawl, now, somehow
holds on to the oak.
The abandoned child returns to recognize her.
They question each other; with some abstract fluttering
two very distinct hands stroke brother Zalman.

—Translated from Spanish by Stephen A. Sadow and J. Kates

Carlos Jacobo Levy

Born in Mendoza, Argentina, Carlos Jacobo Levy (1942–2020) explores Argentine Jewish life in his poems. He is the author of *La memoria y otros poemas* (1984), which took him seventeen years to write, and *Café de náufragos* (1991). Levy was friends with Marcos Silber, with whom he cowrote *Bajo continuo* (2008.) Levy was also advisor to Mendoza's Ministry of Culture and directed Radio Nacional Mendoza. In 2005 Levy, a Sephardic Jew, published a translation into Ladino of José Hernández's classic *The Gaucho Martín Fierro*.

L'CHAIM

If I say *l'chaim*, I toast life
for the whole planet,
for the air that contains it, contains me, and contains
all that lives and that I love.
I say *l'chaim* and I lift my cup for the birds,
doves, blackbirds, sparrows,
condors of powerful flight, wise owls, and
architect ovenbirds.
And if I say *l'chaim*,
I speak of fish, insects, cetaceans, and reptiles.
I remember the biblical whale of Jonah and the mythological
seahorse.
The tadpole of the pond without history after
the storm.
The centipede, the bee, and the lion,
the dog, the cat, and the lizard.
I say *l'chaim* and I live with all that lives.
L'chaim to the plants,
to the life of the lustful tree of the jungle, and to the life
of the needy and heroic bush that survives the
desert.

(I am the one who remembers.
I toast the shade of that willow that wept,
protecting my adolescence and that prohibited love
at siesta time.)
If I say *l'chaim*, it's for sure that I speak of the rain.
I say a toast to it and for the wind that spreads the pollen,
and to the pollen, to the life of the wheat and to its ears.
To the ears of wheat and for the bread

that the father divides for the only meal of the day,
and I say *l'chaim* to the tree of bread dreamed of
                by those who wait
and to the day when those who wait rouse
in the land of milk and honey.
L'chaim, l'chaim, l'chaim, three times for the wine
that lets loose embraces in man,
peoples the taverns with songs and memories
of open hearts as in a beautiful fable.
I will gulp down a larger drink and say *l'chaim*
for those who are far from their hometown
                and shed a tear for it,
so that they may sing their love song tonight
and not feel like strangers in my home.
L'chaim, l'chaim for men's hearts
and to the men who speak the language of that heart.
L'chaim to those who later will be men, children.
To the circle of children: *l'chaim* to the circle of life, and to us.

—Translated from Spanish by Stephen A. Sadow and J. Kates

AY, ANTONIO, ONCE AGAIN ONCE MORE BUT NO

To Rabbi Alejandro Block

"Once again once more like three thousand years ago"
—ANTONIO ESTEBAN AGÜERO

Ay, Antonio, once again once more but no.
Like Homer three thousand years ago,
he dreamt of birds workers ships and words in the plazas.

Once again once more as scarcely
eight hundred thirty-nine short days
since hatred revealed itself in Buenos Aires
on a street like any street of any street at all
where children walk,
men with a simple appetite for hard bread
plodding to work.

Women thinking of their midday soup
and lovers prowling the future:
a street
where perhaps a nun was passing with a nearly unworldly step,
a dance praying her equation of rosaries.
A rabbi,
his tired walk entangling memory in his sidelocks,
a florist a carnation a magnolia
a cat a dog a fish in its fishbowl
swirling its innocence in the water.

On that street, Antonio, hatred spewed from an up-
roar that morning filling the air with fear.

And this time it was not like
three thousand years ago,
when Homer told of life and another uproar
celebrated in the plaza.
Antonio,
once again once more my tranquil café
has been transformed into a huddle of terror,
and I see how my name,
the old names of the old Bible
come together to burn in death with Hernández,
Fernández
Abdala
Marinetti Buttini Di Tarranto Da Souza Van der Heusen
and I believe I have forgotten Homer and his men
birds and ships,
because once again once more I now remember Treblinka
Dachau
Auschwitz
Bosnia Vietnam Korea, the humiliated
isolated and those always victimized.
The helpless and forgotten pariahs
the street kids of Rio waiting for the death
squadrons
while the useless question of why hangs in the air
every time a new day begins.
But I am Jewish, Antonio.
And I was already here before Homer.
The day after tomorrow once more
once again once more I will remember
that three thousand years ago
he launched ships birds workers and words into the plazas.

—Translated from Spanish by Stephen A. Sadow and J. Kates

Ricardo Feierstein

Born in Buenos Aires, Ricardo Feierstein (1942–) is a poet, novelist, essayist, and architect. Hailed as one of the most important Argentine Jewish writers, he has published the books of poetry *La balada del sol* (1969), *Inventadiario* (1972), and *Letras en equilibrio* (1975), and a bilingual anthology, *Las edades* (The Ages) (2004). He was awarded a Buenos Aires Municipal Prize in Literature for his trilogy of novels, *Sinfonía inocente* (1984). He has long been a major force in Argentina's literary scene. His more than thirty works include the narratives *Mestizo* (1994), *Homicidios tímidos* (1996), *La logia del umbral* (2001), *Consorcio Utopía* (2007), *Las novias perdidas* (2011), and *El caso del concurso literario* (2013). His works have been translated into English, French, Italian, and German.

NATIONALITY

Born in Buenos Aires in 1942,
where my first love
came early, the slide of the rain, a fight
where I decked the other guy,
the Peronist anthem from loudspeakers on the street,
triple features for a buck, asthmatic kites,
the first television on the block,
uniforms and horses, excitement and multitudes,
the motley colors of my football club.
I carved a heart on my school desk.
Best in class, I attended Evita's funeral.
I could focus the cold eyeglasses of night
to pass through trees, prostitutes, noises, fiestas,
mirrors of light when my children's eyes bloom.
I looked at the sum—a concertina in the dusk
to scale mountains, to enfold dawns.
I bear this land in my blood.

Born in Buenos Aires in 1942,
the very year
a thousand or a hundred thousand or a million or several million
were converted to flaring columns of smoke
and blackened the German and Polish skies.
How many never-to-be brothers and friends
of mine were already there?
And more, I learned, I learned that red flames and praise
eradicate the hair of the night.
An ancient chronicle overwhelmed my senses,
drew a blue canticle on my ancestral map
in my veins, and I came across the word Jew,

made it dance, dream of feathers, seed the wind,
roll down highways like a runaway wheel
to rejoin its salt and its trembling,
and I follow it by fits and starts.
I bear this echo in my blood.

Born in Buenos Aires in 1942,
on the eighth day I was circumcised.

—Translated from Spanish by Stephen A. Sadow and J. Kates

NOSTALGIA

I'm not willing, not yet willing
to set aside my past or my moods,
nor the wide contentment of a far river
and navigate from the center to the bank
without acknowledging myself tall, Jewish, American.
I'm not willing, no, to dust off melancholies.
I'm not, not in the habit
of shaking out nostalgia as I go along
like a lock of hair across the brow
or a wooly dog after the bath
throwing off cloudbursts like boomerangs.
I'm not willing, no, to live in the past.
I'm not saying, I'm not saying now
that a man is the sum of his memories,
but they do whisper rumors of the future.
They collect life in an open barrel
like blood pumping and pulsing.
I'm not saying, no, that it excludes.
Instead it adds substance.

—Translated from Spanish by Stephen A. Sadow and J. Kates

DISTINGUISHING CHARACTERISTICS

Amazement of being alive.
A heart as big as *this.*
A touch of selfishness.

—Translated from Spanish by Stephen A. Sadow and J. Kates

Hjalmar Flax

Born in San Juan, Puerto Rico, where he still resides, Hjalmar Flax (1942–) studied literature at the University of Pennsylvania and the University of Puerto Rico. He earned a law degree from the latter and practiced law from 1970 to 1998. In addition to working as a film critic, Flax is the author of twelve published books of poems, including *44 Poems* (1969), *Dangerous Confines* (1987), *Large Reasons* (1995), *Contraocaso* (2007), *Penultimatum* (2015) and *50-ODD POEMS* (2017). Flax has received awards from the Institute of Puerto Rican Literature, the PEN Club of Puerto Rico, the Institute of Puerto Rican Culture, and the newspaper *El Nuevo Día*. His work has been translated into English, Romanian, and French.

TENACITY

Everyone carries himself on his own back
through the ups and down of his own existence,
in the rhythm of days and nights,
from week to week, from year to year.
In his small rut,
three or four steps, his routine
dissipates in a short time to nothing.
And yet he lives, as every being lives
its own minuscule existence.
Life has a quality that the creature does not know
and without knowing carries on: the crab in its cave,
the insect in its tree, the embedded barnacle,
the earthworm, the bird, the fish, the goat . . .
Life has something that comes now and then.
But man, haughty,
with his swollen, delirious ganglia,
thinks he is different from the bird, the fish, the goat:
superior to barnacles, earthworms, insects,
freer than the crab on the shore of the sea.
He fantasizes his own existence, rejects his future,
but dies in his time, like everything else.
May I see the essence of each inert being,
the special wonder of each living being
that shares with me this space, this moment,
this air, this light, this destiny.

—Translated from Spanish by Stephen A. Sadow and J. Kates

Ariel Dorfman

Ariel Dorfman (1942–) is a Chilean American author, born in Argentina. Since writing *How to Read Donald Duck* in 1971, he has built up an impressive body of fiction, poetry, memoirs, and nonfiction that has been translated into more than fifty languages. His plays, including *Death and the Maiden* (1992) (later made into a film by Roman Polanski) and *Purgatorio* (2008), have been staged in over one hundred countries. Among his recent books are the novels *Darwin's Ghosts* (2020), *Cautivos* (2020), *The Compensation Bureau* (2021), the children's story *The Rabbits' Rebellion* (2020), and *Voices from the Other Side of Death* (2022), a collection of poems. He and his wife, Angélica, divide their time between Chile and Durham, North Carolina, where he is a distinguished emeritus professor of literature at Duke University.

VOCABULARY

1

But how can I tell their story
if I was not there?

When two of them met
far away
on an unfamiliar street corner,
they could not know if it was
a first meeting
or a farewell.
They could not know who was looking at them
from the quadrangle
of that window.
Reporting every movement,
every movement of their lips.

I was looking at them from another country,
and I cannot tell their story.
I was calling from another country,
and the phone was always busy.

2

Show me a word I can use.
Show me one verb.
An adjective as clear as a ray of light.
Listen carefully to the bottom of each sentence,
to the attic and the dust in the furniture
of every sentence.

Perk up your ears.
Listen and look under the bed
of every sentence
at the soldiers waiting their turn
at the foot
of the bride's bed.

To preserve just one word.
What is it to be?
Like a question in a quiz show.
If you could take one word with you
to the future,
what is it to be?
Find it.
Plunge into the garbage heap.
Stick your hands deep into the ooze.
Close your fist around the fragment of a mirror
fractured by feet that dance on what should have been
a wedding night.
Let me tell you something.
Even if I had been there
I could not have told their story.

3

I was calling from another country,
and the phone was always busy.
I was trying to call home,
and the machine had just swallowed
my last dime.

4

As to the story I cannot tell,
they accumulated tenderness
as others accumulate money.
Ask them.
Even if the phone is busy.
Even if the machine has just swallowed your last dime.
Even if the operator drowns out all the other voices.
Ask them for the verse our lovers will still need
if we are ever again to bathe
in the same river.

Let them speak for themselves.

—Written in English by the author

Gloria Gervitz

In 1979 Gloria Gervitz (1943–2022), born in Mexico City, published *Shajarit,* an experimental piece that began her life-long project *Migraciones* (Migrations). She then wrote *Fragmento de Ventana* (1986), *Yiskor* (1987), *Pythia* (1993), *Treno* (2003), and *Septiembre* (2003). Starting in 2002 she again turned to *Migraciones* and published a series of new editions, each incorporating new sections. She continued to make revisions and alterations to the text until it was finally completed as one continuous work without section titles in 2020. She has translated poets such as Clarice Lispector, Samuel Beckett, and Anna Akhmatova. Her work has been translated into French, Hebrew, Italian, Japanese, Portuguese, Russian, and German. In 2019 Gloria Gervitz was awarded the very prestigious Pablo Neruda Ibero-American Poetry Award from the Cervantes Society. Jewish themes permeate Gervitz's work, often appearing in unexpected places in her poetry.

FROM *MIGRATIONS*

let the word come to you
let it signify the name
let it be dark and quiet
the name does not name itself
it is named by its presence
by its echo its resonance
the name is not spoken
let the word flow
let it see into the blood
let it bleed out within you
don't try to understand it
don't question it
let it be
let it born
let it beat
mute as the name of God
wash it bath it sanctify it
she is one leading you to her
look her in the face
she is inside you
know that she is blessed
know that she is not the fruit of your womb
know that she is in everyone and belongs to no one
know that she has blessed you
. . .
    kneading of light
                river mouth
        brightness
                        as if her heart had
          failed

as it is in God

and there I am
like someone watching
like someone listening
I am the intruder
the one you foretold
wait
and tremble
that human trembling
in your presence
and there's no air

ah, you who I've
been waiting for

in your joy
I ask for
that which satisfied
satisfies

who is that
who makes me
who
I am

and what for
and why
am I?

—Translated from Spanish by Mark Schafer

Isaac Goldemberg

Born in Peru, Isaac Goldemberg (1945–) lives in New York but maintains close ties to his native country. His books include *Libro de las transformaciones* (2007), *Acuérdate del escorpión* (2010), *La vida breve* (2012), and *Diálogos conmigo y mis otros* (2013). In 2001 his novel *The Fragmented Life of Don Jacobo Lerner* was selected by the National Yiddish Book Center as one of the 100 most important Jewish books of the last 150 years. Goldemberg was Distinguished Professor of Humanities at Hostos Community College of the City University of New York. His poetry is syncretic and freely mixes Jewish, Christian, and Indigenous themes.

INEXACT SONNET OF THE PERUVIAN JEW AND VICE VERSA

Jesus, you have forgotten my America,
come be born one day in these crazy lands.

—CARLOS PELLICER

For God's sake, don't even dream, Jesus,
of being born in my other promised land.
On bended knee this Jew implores you,
as well as this Peruvian who flays me

for being the son of a camel. No, a burro!
A burro offered up on your wooden cross
with which this Jew flogs me, in vain,
for being the inexact son of burro and camel.

Jesus, pay no attention to the poet who summons you
from the abyss of his Christian being
to be born in these crazy lands.

By the God of Abraham, in you I trust
that you will not render my Peruvian
what you have given abundantly to my Jew.

—Translated from Spanish by Stephen A. Sadow and J. Kates

YOM KIPPUR

(Chacra Colorada, 1955)

The synagogue is partying:
ladies adorned with medieval jewels
show off their Diaspora furs
men with little purple caps
—heads infested with numbers and letters—
cluster like flies
around the Ark of the Covenant
All the while old Jews with ashen beards
skulk through the streets of Lima
their stomachs fasting
knowing that this is the day
God inscribes in His Account Book
with His own fist and letter
the souls to be saved or damned
They arrive punctually at the doorway of the temple
(memory flees them over bridges and
through deserts)
The rabbi sounds the immemorial horn
The old men hold hands
lower their heads
enter in like ghosts

—Translated from by Stephen A. Sadow and J. Kates

Manuela Fingueret

The daughter of Lithuanian Jewish immigrants, Manuela Fingueret (1945–2013) was an Argentine writer and journalist. In 1993 she was director of Buenos Aires's FM Jai, the most important Jewish radio station in Latin America. From 2000 to 2004 she was general director of the Public Libraries Network of the City of Buenos Aires. She then assumed the position as head of the Directorate of Books and the Promotion of Reading of Buenos Aires. Her books of poetry include *Heredarás Babel* (1977), *La piedra es una llaga en el tiempo* (1980), *Ciudad en fuga y otros infiernos* (1984), *Los huecos de tu cuerpo* (1992), *Uva y racimo* (1998), and *Esquina* (2001). Her novels are *Blues de la calle Leiva* (1995), *Hija del silencio* (2006), and *Ajo para el diablo* (2011). Fingueret's poetry reflects on memory and barbarism, the Holocaust, and dictatorships in Latin America.

SECOND PORTRAIT

I am the whistling of the night
that flees before the bird of prey
in a boat run aground.

A sphere that rests
in a tree by Magritte
and savagely rushes in
at the call of the master
when he smells rain in his armpits.

A fleeting movement
before the siesta
when the cobweb
weave glances into the skin.

I am a pirate of constant boardings
who smells homemade bread
and profanes it with a scream
until the skins are devoured
—peaceful apple with colors on its body—

A fragile cord
that floats without fright
or a panther that frightens the unprepared
and devours him in small vibrations
to enjoy the ritual.
Each time his blood is a sacrifice.

I am the survivor of prayers and exterminations
in a Lithuanian village
that still burns in memory.

A purple enchantress
to whom they recite psalms
and who does not wish to awaken
because morning is so white
and enchantment so brief
that a flash of light can stir her.

I am an arrow in the universe
that trembles when a child grows
and whose destiny
is a golden mantle of dry leaves
in an ascendant point of the Milky Way.

—Translated from Spanish by Roberta Gordenstein

EACH MORNING MAKING SURE

Each morning making sure
that nobody leaves their internal life without effort.
Protecting yourself from the yellow wall
that supports your vertical patience above the other three
—without being important to you, of course—
and you fall.
Reversing the poles of affection
toward the geranium petals
that overload your patience
in the old, abandoned courtyards of candor.
Confirming like a hard-working ant
the letters of your own alphabet,
bringing them back to their origin in sounds and structure.
Humming until the chords of fury,
until you get weary
—what difference does it make—
transforming them into exhausting seed,
stubborn and rootless.
Dividing nostalgia
into exactly equal parcels,
enjoying each one
—flawlessly—
like obstacles to get over every sleepless night.
Tying yourself to madness, braiding it with care
—hair by hair—
to the true story of yourself,
the one without epitaphs,
that lies hidden and haunting,
hoping that word of its love
is unique and will prepare it
for the final shock of not being able to act with kindness.

—Translated from Spanish by Stephen A. Sadow and J. Kates

Evelyn Wertheimer

Born in Montevideo, Uruguay, Evelyn Wertheimer (1945–) studied under Professor Silvia Lago and the Uruguayan poets Jorge Arbeleche, Washington Benavídes, and Rafael Courtoisie. Her books include *Teshuvá* (1997) and *Adagio* (2022), the latter a volume of haiku.

OF COURSE THE STREETS AND THE HOUSES

of course the streets and the houses
of course the plazas and the people
but not always the gesture of the dawn
pretense   alternation
bloody game in which a goodbye
is forever
of course, yes, I have seen them
and the luckless daughters and the sons
I have seen them passing
as the dawn tends to watch us

—Translated from Spanish by Stephen A. Sadow

Bella Clara Ventura

Born in Bogotá, Colombia, to Jewish parents, Bella Clara Ventura (1947–) studied in Paris. A director, screenwriter, and film producer, she has published twelve collections of poems, among them *Diáspora y asombro* (1996), *La niña de adentro* (2002), *Árboles de leche y miel* (2009), and *Antología poética* (2018). Her novels include *Almamocha* (1993), *El viento de la sombra* (2003), *Contigo aprendí* (2007), and *Canadá para siempre* (2020). She has been awarded first place in the Dios Mío Contest in Israel (2011), first prize in Wings of Poetry in Chile (2012), and the Rosetta Poetry Prize in Turkey (2013). Bella Clara Ventura is honorary president of the Hispano-American Union of Letters. She lives in Israel.

BLIND FAITH

To my little sister Ana Mercedes Vivas

Without fear of the unknown
I take on risks,
as many as possible.
And I take the chance
that they call me
stupid or gullible.
I confess I trust in the day to day.
The One Above is familiar with what awaits me.
He gives in easy installments
the value of interior growth,
perhaps full of pains,
but at the end as a good reward
I know that I have done my duty
to learn from the here and now.
True meaning of life.
Fluidity in its maximum expression
as channel of bliss
in the bends of trouble.
They disrupt existence
to love again
the blind faith
when the eye sees
with a heart without limit.

—Translated from Spanish by Stephen A. Sadow and J. Kates

Tamara Kamenzsain

Tamara Kamenszain (1947–2021) was born in Buenos Aires and attended the University of Buenos Aires. Kamenszain received the poetry prize of the National Arts Fund of Argentina for *De este lado del Mediterráneo* (1973), her first book of poems. Kamenszain taught at the University of Buenos Aires and the University of Mexico and worked for the National Endowment for the Arts in Mexico and the Ministry of Culture in Argentina. She was a prolific author whose critical works include *El texto silencioso* (1983) and *El libro de Tamar* (2018). Her poetry, such as *La casa grande* (1986), *Tango bar* (1998), *El Ghetto* (2003), and *Solos y solas* (2005), is known for its mix of autobiography and reflection. She wrote about her mourning for her father and her mother's affliction with Alzheimer's disease. Kamenszain is the recipient of a Guggenheim Fellowship and the Pablo Neruda Presidential Medal.

I HAVE NEVER TOLD THIS TO ANY OF MY ANALYSTS

I HAVE NEVER TOLD THIS to any of my analysts.
In Jewish elementary school every year we watched
the same movie of Nazi concentration camps,
that one where some living cadavers dig the ditch
they then throw the bones of their dead into,
and later they are compelled
to push themselves into suicide by others
who shoot them so they fall lightly,
without food or drink.
I don't know why, but still today when a taxi driver says
something about Jews I go quiet
so he won't notice
in the rearview mirror
that I am at the edge of that ditch.
That's why I don't volunteer opinions, why I hide
behind the first person.

—Translated from Spanish by Stephen A. Sadow and J. Kates

SEATED AT THE EDGE OF HER MEMORY

SEATED AT THE EDGE OF her memory
I file myself away in functioning oblivion
words between us are cut short
she doesn't speak and I stop saying what I was saying
I stopped speaking so as not to embarrass her
together we go on creating a temporary present
in that early moment my mother remains alone
because I am like the fools I choose to follow
I believe that in the future everything is waiting for me
while no one gives her hope
so separated we go on together
she who heard my birth sits me on the edge
to make me listen to the anticipation of her death
our shared pasts come and go
receding futures come and go
she doesn't know what I don't know she asks me, what do I do?
I answer her eat get dressed sleepwalk sit down
the chirping of her robot cares for her today
that minimalism that I will have to reprogram tomorrow.

—Translated from Spanish by Stephen A. Sadow and J. Kates

Luis Kleiman

Born in San José, Costa Rica, Luis Kleiman (1948–1999) studied at the National Autonomous University of Mexico and the University of Costa Rica. He worked as a journalist at Radio Monumental for its *The Word of Costa Rica* program and was a correspondent for newspapers in Brazil. His books include *Mis primeros salmos* (1970), *Opus cero: sinfonía teórica* (1982), *Ritual salubre* (1988), and *Meditaciones y creencias* (1998). Kleiman also authored a two-volume study on the history of Sephardic Jews.

III LOGIC

To Samuel Rovinski, friend of literature

The opposition of the magnets,
divided, separated
in its dissident poles,
causes the annulment of the forces.

And in the nucleus
the movement balanced
by inertia
decreases to its death,
to the multiplication of the words.

—Translated from Spanish by Stephen A. Sadow

Becky Rubinstein F.

Born in Mexico City, poet, teacher, translator, cultural journalist, and promoter of children's literature Becky Rubinstein F. (1949–) studied at the National Autonomous University of Mexico, where she was a professor of medieval Spanish literature between 1986 and 1994. Her many awards include the Gabino Barreda Medal and the Sor Juana Medal. Her books include *Las divinas mutantes* (1996) and the anthology *34 poetas mexicanos de las pirámides* (2005) in addition to dozens of children's books.

EVE VI

seats her man at the table,
          serves him the specialty of the house.

Apples in all their forms:
roasted,
          boiled
                    sliced
                              in syrup
                                        in a pie.

It is said that the apple is multifaceted,
          fruit of a thousand faces.

However, it showed no face
when God exiled the ill-fated first
          gourmets from paradise.

—Translated from Spanish by Stephen A. Sadow and J. Kates

EVE VIII

Eve knew she was the cosmic mother.
And this worried her.

To carry the world on her belly,
her responsibility that of an Atlas.
To wander roads through the world
like Saint Christopher.

Saddened, she sits at the threshold of her dwelling
and weeps for the death of one son
          and the damnation of the other.

And she weeps for all the dead,
for all the suffering
          of the children of her children.

Cosmic mother, she accepts her fate and spreads out through
the doorframe of all ages.

—Translated from Spanish by Stephen A. Sadow and J. Kates

Daniel Samoilovich

Daniel Samoilovich (1949–) was born in Buenos Aires, where he studied at the National Academy. He began working for *Clarín* newspaper in 1969. In 1978 he traveled to Spain and worked as editor of the magazine *Triunfo* and the newspaper *El País*. In 1979 Samoilovich codirected with Gloria Pampillo Madrid's magazine *La construcción imaginaria*. Later on he returned to Buenos Aires. His numerous books of poetry include *Las encantadas* (2003), *El carrito de Eneas* (2003), and *Molestando a los demonios* (2009). His poetry is often whimsical about things Jewish.

A FABLE ABOUT THE ORIGIN OF MAN

The evening of the Sixth Day was coming on.
God checked his list:
"Waters above the celestial vault
and waters below the celestial vault, divided.
Hippopotamus: done. Plants, including carnivores:
done. Fruits, fish, puddles,
clouds of mosquitoes above the puddles,
fumaroles opening in the mouths of a volcano,
eels writhing in dry riverbeds,
plovers running scatterbrained along beaches,
land iguanas, slow,
sea iguanas, black,
catatonic in the stones of the coast,
forests, peanuts, sharks: done.
Is there anything missing? Oh yes, those two.
Yes, Night is falling, the night
that I myself created to follow Day.
How tired I am, so many things, what delicate
adjustment of teeth and flesh
vulnerable to those same teeth,
how the shells of tortoises grow
by hexagons, adjusting some with others,
adding some to others, forming
enormous shells
that can't have been born enormous.
Oh, how much chemistry, physics,
geometry, systems design,
chains of hunted and hunters, and the hunted in turn
because hunters in their turn need to have
their own eagle claw.

Night coming on with those two still missing.
Let's see here, a little mud.
Oh, night coming on, I can see nothing.
The Sabbath star is about to appear.
I'll make them now, later we'll see.

—Translated from Spanish by Stephen A. Sadow and J. Kates

Moacir Amâncio

Moacir Amâncio (1949–) is a Brazilian poet, journalist, scholar, and translator. He is a professor of Hebrew language and literature at the University of São Paulo, where he studies Jewish literature and culture and Brazilian literature. He is the author of the poetry collections *Figuras na sala* (1996), *O olho do canário* (1997), *Colores siguientes* (1999), *Ata* (2007), and *Matula* (2016). He is known for his translations from Hebrew of the Israeli writers Amos Oz, Aharon Appelfeld, and Ronny Someck. In his poetry Amâncio recreates the long-lost mosaic of Jewish identity and history in colonial and imperial Brazil that was erased by the Inquisition. His poetry tends toward mysticism. This poem celebrates the thirteenth century French Kabbalist Isaac the Blind, also known ironically as "Saghi Nehor," which means "Much Light" in Aramaic.

SAGHI NEHOR

We aren't in any Dizengoff,
street filled with store windows and doors
full of crooked jellyfish, wild animals
resting in the alleyways, strays.
No small boat approaches
from any island, from any dead.
A shadow of whoever spreads shade
climbs on the thin skin
the fragrant color of yellow-silver,
and it is only that lunar smell that stays on,
prohibited the touch, gesture nevertheless
combined in a place
all lit up, but blind
the alphabet of the cloven hooves
always hypothesis of passageways
turned off in the blue breath.
Remainder of landscape, traces of the look,
a peculiar way to say apple.

—Translated from Portuguese by Regina Igel

Irene Gruss

Born in Buenos Aires, Irene Gruss (1950–2018) was part of a poetry workshop with Mario Jorge de Lellis, Jorge Aulicino, and Daniel Freidemberg. She wrote for magazines like *El escarabajo de oro* and *El ornitorrinco*. In 1975 Gruss received the First Prize for Unpublished Poetry from the Municipality of the City of Buenos Aires. Among her poetry books are *La luz en la ventana* (1982), *Sobre el asma* (1995), *La mitad de la verdad: Obra poética reunida 1982–2007* (2008), and *Entre la pena y la nada* (2015). Her powerful short novel *Una letra familia* (2017) describes in poetic prose the childhood of a middle-class Jewish girl in Buenos Aires. This poem deals with Argentina's Dirty War.

MEANWHILE

I was washing clothes
while many people
disappeared
just like that
hid
suffered
there were blows
and
now they aren't here
just like that
and while sirens and shots, dry sound
passed by
I was washing clothes,
rocking,
I was singing,
and the darkened window blinds.

—Translated from Spanish by Stephen A. Sadow and J. Kates

Susana Grimberg

Susana Grimberg (1950–) is a poet, writer, psychoanalyst, and columnist. She is a contributor to *Comunidades,* an independent Jewish newspaper. Her theoretical contributions as a psychoanalyst were published by the Freudian School of Argentina. She has extensive experience in radio and is host of the popular show *A la vuelta.* She has written the novels *Refugios en la ciudad* (1995), *El espejo de las palabras* (1998), and *Melodía interrumpida* (2013). Her poetry includes *Los bordes del tiempo* (2002), *La mirada de Ana* (2005), *Sinfonía Mayor* (2009), and *Geometría de la libertad* (2014). Her book of short stories, *Relatos completos,* was published in 2016. In the following poems Susana Grimberg writes about Anne Frank and the biblical Eve.

FIRST

was to leave behind the business, then the bicycle,
then the school,
then the movies,
then the car,
then the tram.
Then the clothing.
                Then life.
                        Then

—Translated from Spanish by Stephen A. Sadow and J. Kates

EVE

My whole body aches with love.

—JORGE LUIS BORGES

A woman,
Adam's dream,
left him cut open.

She was the wound,
he will woo her.

A woman, part
of him.
The man will seek her.
Always.

They will never know where they are.

She will desire him
and will lose herself
with him.

He will lose himself
in her.

A woman has slept through the cloudless night.
The body awakens from the other body.

One of them, burning and sleepless, breathes her desire.
The other, burning and wakeful, spurs his desire.

He sleeps through the day instead of the night.
What time does the Sun show its face?

She paces along the clay paths.
She listens, she frets, crosses silence, surprise.

She returns to herself,
she pulls him from his sleep

to show herself to his being,
at that moment
dug into the emptiness.
A hiss
slides itself,

arises.

A standing form among the trees.

Serpent.

Whispers tempt caresses.

Fascinates.

It is only a hiss.
Long.
Suspended in the air.

Seduces.

She wants to stroke him.

Naked.

A chance look.

Words that desire to know of a desire closer than skin.

The words are the other.

The other seduces,
rises,
hypnotizes.

The hiss is that other.

The other:
the occasion.

She wants to know,
know the liquor of Adam's body,
know the taste,
know the passion,
know the desire.

The other's pleasure is unknowable,
known,
savored.

The woman whom thou hast drawn from my body
tempted me, he said.
The fruit forbidden (to the man)
was pleasing to my sight, she said.

The forbidden:
to know beyond the silence.

Shame
clothed their bodies.
Insinuating vine leaves
keep catching the eye.

They contrived disguise, obstacle,
seduction.
Playing hide-and-seek,
they left behind the gardens of the immeasurable.

They imagined a sword
to adorn the gate.
Brilliant metal.
Dazzling, without return.
Exiles from sweet ignorance.

To choose.
To choose to err.
To err,
to err forever.

To know the knowledge,
the bitter sweetness of curiosity.

—Translated from Spanish by Stephen A. Sadow and J. Kates

Juana García Abás

Juana García Abás (1950–) is a Spanish-Cuban writer born in Havana of Sephardic descendants. A member of the prestigious Union of Writers and Artists of Cuba, she works as a journalist, art critic, and playwright. In her first poetry works, she was guided by the world-renowned writers José Lezama Lima and Roque Dalton. In 2006 García Abás won the Nicolás Guillén National Poetry Prize, one of Cuba's most important literary honors, for her book-length collection *Circunloquio* (2006). In 2022 she received the Cuban National Culture Distinction Medal. The Cuban critic Juan Losada has written: "Juana García Abás assembles the porticoes and sews the veils like those in the Ark of the Covenant." García Abás's poetry is often hermetic, always philosophical, and integrates symbols from world culture. Her Jewish poetry is highly influenced by her knowledge of the Kabbalah and quantum physics.

TESTIMONY

for José Kozer

When the aleph precedes the letter of the name . . .
—SÉFER YETZIRÁ

I wait for conjunctions of change and permanence,
I shower guesses on my leaves of mastic
and record litanies in red resin
asking for acorns from a pear tree
with the indifference of the ubiquitous.
The letters of my name are myself.
I redeem the misery of this sphere
undoing fissures,
cracking universes against the dark.
A trial by ordeal stirs up the lees
of the angel we keep losing track of,
his exile's flight into the ephemeral,
and brings forth a swaying uncertainty
—moldering root and offshoot of the phoenix—
pursuing the eternally postponed goal
of this thirst that recurs beside the fountain.
(The labyrinth corrupts its vortices
—with no above or below, nothing comes or goes—
thoughtlessness undermines tabernacles.
No luck is predestined or land foreordained.
The encoding of this black light
negates the sparks of these smashed pitchers.
No wizard discovers that nothingness is a myth,
and the entrails of Adam Cadmus find the miracle

of this paradox that God did not choose.)
Heretical or messianic, I believe I am anointed
with something more vital than my ochre oils.
On the eve of a holy day, I abandon odds and ends.
Now I construct canopies to defeat devils:
the face of a tesseract in my changing signs,
this bread without yeast in the honey of your hands,
and the branch of Æneas in the blessed guano.

—Translated from Spanish by Stephen A Sadow and J. Kates

TEXTUS

The idea of the possible sings and relates,
the root of which nothing can be preached,
with its walnut nuclei behind four parchments
of black fire on white fire.
Because what is below is above.
What is inside is outside,
and something that belongs where everything changes
in an endless chain, as the ant
lifting a mustard seed
forces a schism in Alpha Centauri,
while the flora of the revelations foretells,
before the panic of the prelates,
grace for mystics and scourge for the prophet.

—Translated from Spanish by Stephen A Sadow and J. Kates

ABOUT ORDERED CHAOS

Stop, you are so beautiful!
—GOETHE

The infinite sustains its exiles,
its chapters in expansion
—and there is no ultimate limit,
ultimate moment, nor ultimate being.
The turmoil embodies its boundaries deferred.

—Translated from the Spanish by Stephen A. Sadow J. Kates

Nora Strejilevich

After being freed from a concentration camp during Argentina's Dirty War, Nora Strejilevich (1951–) became a political exile in Canada, where she earned a doctorate in Latin American literature. *Una sola muerte numerosa* (2001), awarded the Letras de Oro International Prize, was translated into English as *A Single Numberless Death* (2002), adapted to theater, and inspired the Italian docufiction film *Nora* (2005). She has taught at San Diego State University, the University of Chile, and the National University of Tres de Febrero in Buenos Aires.

WHEN THEY ROBBED ME OF NAME

I was one of a hundred, out of thousands,
and I was no one.
Deprived of gesture, gaze, and voice,
my face was reduced to the letters NN.

In my numbered nakedness I walk
alone with them
in eyeless and selfless rows
through guttural chains,
through civic wailing of a country
without initials.

Eyelid and partitions
my horizon
all silence and echo
all bars all night
all mirrorless wall
nowhere to copy a wrinkle
a grimace a perhaps

All a full stop and a moving on.

Until one day
they gave me back my name,
and I went out to display it through the hallways
of the world.
I found masks,
countries' drowsy profiles,
tongues greedy for news,
the absurd.

I let myself walk like this
toward my nowhere
toward my nothingness
through steep paths of
dewless bones
unable to translate
my scars.

That name is not mine!
Mine

was a hundred was a thousand was everyone's
mine
was body being womb was voice
had neighbors whistled
was diurnal and nocturnal
was a god.

I've lost my name!
I shouted through the trails of a
cornerless map
between doors riddled with fear.

I want my name!
my own curved, throbbing name.
Bring it to me!
Wrapped in spring
with an *r* for *rayuela*
and an *o* for *ojalá*
and *a* for *aserrín aserrán*

My curling name got tangled
between death syllables
DI SAP PEAR ED
gone
a name never again
my name.

Alienated from my subject,
I didn't know how to conjugate myself
or how to navigate
the *abc*'s of my tears.

I was eyes looking back upon yesterdays
I was hands snatching at rags
I was feet slipping
through electric lines.

I didn't know how to express myself.
I was skin between
dry and vacuous speeches
without saliva without vestiges,
with not why or wherefore,

no whensoever or whereupon.
You will never be able to say it!
never speak for yourself, I thought.

But you will write.
Yes, I will write
thousands of *G*s of *R*s of *S*s
vicarious scribbles,
offspring rising from my mouth

whirlpools of desires
that once were names.

I will inscribe
black whips to tame
other wild capital letters
drowning my blood.
With first and last names
I will resist you will resist
the brazen language
self-oblivion.

—Translated from Spanish by Celeste Kostopulos Cooperman

NN: No Name
rayuela: hopscotch
aserrín aserrán: popular children's nursery rhyme

Perla Sneh

A psychoanalyst, writer, researcher, and a literary translator of Yiddish, Perla Sneh (1952–) received a doctorate from the University of Buenos Aires. She is a senior researcher at the Center for Genocide Studies at the National University of Tres de Febrero. Her book *Palabras para decirlo: Lenguaje y exterminio* (2012, 2022) was awarded the National Prize by Argentina's Ministry of Culture. Her books of poetry are *Ciudad autónoma* (2004), *Bíblicos* (2006), *Jarabe de pico* (2011), and *Palabras para decirlo* (2012).

AND HE SAID TO ABRAHAM, SEND AWAY THAT SERVANT

and he said to Abraham, send away that servant
and her son since the son of that servant will not inherit together with my *son*

At the hour, he murmured, for the man fulfilled by day, dawn is a blessing; but the patriarch tended to the sand; and the woman who will have to depart; with her, her son; with her, his son and she who will stay; with her, her son; and how long the water in his wineskin will last; the woman takes the hand of her child who is no longer a child; it pains her to remember that she didn't want that child born for another; it pains her the punishment that he inherited; it pains her to know that now he has to leave. She loves him, she says in her heart; he is beautiful as only a dream can be; the sun, the sun, the man, and the sand become quiet; the desert is stingy with love; she lets go of his hand, the boy, and watch; he won't have to move until midday; she hears the weeping of the child who sleeps and says in her heart, he is beautiful as only a dream can be; but at that hour the woman sits on the rock and the child lies on the sand; she dreams a weeping that is not of children but of the wineskin that bleeds its last drop; the woman does not want to look at the child who is no longer a child; the boy doesn't know that messenger approaches; and the man looks for in his old man's mouth the shout that will quicken the steps of the angel and open the child's eyes. Although perhaps it wasn't more than the wind never light in the scriptures.

—Translated from Spanish by Stephen A. Sadow

Sandro Cohen

Poet, writer, editor, translator, and teacher Sandro Cohen (1953–2020) was born in Newark, New Jersey, and studied at Rutgers University. A Mexican citizen since 1982, he taught writing at the Metropolitan Autonomous University, Azcapotzalco. As an editor he launched the Crack Generation (made up of writers Jorge Vopi, Ignacio Padilla, and Eloy Urroz, among others) and founded Editorial Colibrí, among other cultural endeavors. His books include *Los cuerpos de la furia* (1983), *Línea de fuego* (1989), and *Corredor nocturno* (1995). Cohen's passion for the Spanish language was enormous, as is clear from his work on the popular manual of style *Redacción sin dolor* (2015). When he contracted COVID-19 at the beginning of the pandemic, a massive crowdfunding campaign was orchestrated to cover his medical expenses.

THIS, IN ESSENCE, ENDED . . .

This, in essence, ended.
It began a long time ago, I know,
but for a while now I don't feel
immortal. And when I'm no longer here,
napkins will stay in the same place on the table,
the same cars will park
in the same spots, more or less,
with the same levels of that anguish,
so Mexican and deep,
but I won't see them any longer
from this table with a green cloth,
seated in this chair
of unyielding plastic
that lets me be easy,
reading the news.
I still won't understand, half a meter
from a sidewalk where ladies stroll
with their dogs and children,
where they carefully put out their trash
bags for the truck coming on time
with its intolerable
little bell, but I
no long think of complaining,
nor do I cover my ears:
simply and modestly, I won't be here.
And it is hard to get used to
the solid idea of my absence,
but it is palpable, as palpable
as a young girl's breasts, or her lips,
or her manner of asking me

to pay attention to her, but how,
if I'll no longer be here?
These words that write themselves
will be my testament; they will affirm
what I have finally understood:
we are on earth only a little while,
but it is all there is, as I have been everyone,
and among everything we write
the words that are urgently needed,
those that slip away,
that we have always spoken.

—Translated from Spanish by Stephen A. Sadow and J. Kates

Rubén Ackerman

Rubén Ackerman (1954–2017) studied psychology and sociology at the Central University of Venezuela. He was coauthor of the poetic anthology *El ojo errante* (2009) for the group of the same name. His poems appear in the anthology *102 poetas: Jamming* (2015). *Los ausentes* (2016), his only single-author book of poetry, was awarded the Illustrious Prize of the City of Cuenca, Ecuador. Ackerman's poetry calls for persistence and patience in hard times.

YOU HAVE TO TURN THE PAGE

You have to turn the page
recover the lost gesture of those who are not here
be the editors of epitaphs
You have to feel beyond our instability
(Our daily bread)
raise your hands even without faith resuscitate our dead
You have to learn to hallucinate in full daylight
be able to see what nobody sees
You have to recover our ration of faith
our plate of soup for the needy
We have to turn ourselves to stone
(It is written in the Talmud)
so the absent faces of our dead
may be seen in our eyes
You have to return to the desert
become mute in the sand
restore the ancient pact between the living and the dead
You have to turn the page

—Translated by Stephen A. Sadow and J. Kates

ARS POETICA

The best thing is to stop time
when the dice are still in the air
about to
fall
and freeze that emotion forever
but God or chance
places destiny on the table
The best thing is to stay suspended

but the clock betrays us
and quickly the man from the electric company
or mother-in-law comes to give us a very wise piece of advice

The best thing is the space between inspiration and expiration

when thoughts become absent
and we are light
hot
innocent
The best thing is when God doubts everything even himself
in the interval between faith and atheism
when the truth folds and unfolds
and we collapse as we rise
The best thing is to remain suspended
in an embrace
without returning to
dust and earth

—Translated from Spanish by Stephen A. Sadow and J. Kates

Marjorie Agosín

Born in Chile, Marjorie Agosín (1955–) is the Andrew W. Mellon Professor in the Humanities at Wellesley College. She began writing poetry as a child, and in 1969 her family moved to Athens, Georgia, where she continued to write poems in Spanish. She received her PhD from Indiana University. Agosín is the author of numerous collections of poetry, among them *Sargasso* (1993), *Toward the Splendid City* (1994), and *On the Threshold of Memory: New and Selected Poems* (2003). In 1995 she was awarded the Latino Literature Prize. Agosín is also the author of several prose works, including *A Cross and a Star: Memoirs of a Jewish Girl in Chile* (1995) and *I Lived on Butterfly Hill* (2015), winner of the International Latino Book Award in fiction for young adults. A prominent human rights activist, Agosín is known for her work promoting social justice and feminism. In 1998 she received a United Nations Leadership Award in Human Rights, and in 2002 the Chilean government awarded her the Gabriela Mistral Award for Life Achievements.

COUSINS

My mother always spoke their names
in murmurs,
Julia, Silvia, Sonia,
Sonia, Julia, Silvia.
These were names of rivers,
names of doomed women.
They were my cousins,
women we had known about,
with whom we shared a story.
I loved them from far away
and from close by.

We knew nothing about them.
Little was known of the stubborn time of the war.
Only certain hints,
a murmur
like a sigh.
They sent us secret instructions
never fulfilled,
false leads,
invisible names.
At all the major holidays
there were empty places.
And my father, raising his consecrated cup,
named them
Julia, Sonia, Silvia.

I too came to hold them dear.
I had to settle for
knowing their handwriting

on tattered postcards
from Vienna, then
Prague, and
then from cities with harsh names.

My grandmother Helena,
tight-lipped,
would take out her photographs that
seemed like amber-colored bones
glowing with absences.
Out of the blue,
after almost fifty
years,
a cousin calls from Sweden
and I was able to stop only remembering them.

He told us,
tongue-tied,
thin among the distances,
that he had seen
those cousins:
Julia, Sonia, Silvia.
He had found them
in the holy book of
the dead.
He had tracked them down
by their surnames and their journeys.

They had been transported in those
trains of shadows
and bald women
singing with their blue dresses

to Terezin
in transit to
Auschwitz
where there is no oblivion,
where there are no calendars,

where there is no memory,
where there is no voice,
where the women are silenced,
have their heads shaved,
go mad,
and make of their heads the ceremonials
of dead birds.
The cousin from Sweden
found them.
They were dead and alive
and had arrived on an amber afternoon
wounded and dead.

He told me quickly
that they killed them with blue gas
and that is all he knows about them.
He told me to tell my mother
and the mother of my mother,
also Aunt Regina.

All of them
in Auschwitz
and I don't know how to call them
and I don't know how to recall them.

Anger mixes with my lamentation.
I recognize them,

Sonia, Julia, Silvia.
I can't name them any longer,
and I see them carved up in those forests
of dead butterflies,
and I think that I don't deserve this life
without them.

I tell my mother
and my grandmother, who has remained in the south,
that we should not be looking for them.
That we don't believe in deceptive signs
that they are here.
That they were burned
upon arrival,
and their little bones were placed
nameless in little ovens
of death.

I grow hazy when telling this story
and I am telling it only in a poem
because I can't tell it to anyone.
I don't want to hear things like,
"Here the Jews go again with their memories."
"That happened years ago."
"I don't know anything about the matter."
They spoke that way when the neighbor disappeared,
the grandfather,
his little grandchildren.
Tonight
it spins and spins in my head
like a bouquet of dead
poppies.

I already know where Julia, Sonia, Silvia are.
I will go to steer my way in those fields.
My passion will kiss those grasses
hoping to find their lips.

Julia, Sonia, Silvia
will not die inside the wire.
They will no longer be the Jews hidden
without hair and without language.

I will return to the camps
to wash them with prayers and consecrated water.
I will give you a notebook, Julia,
a fan, Sonia,
a breath of light, Silvia.
My cousins, my sisters, cousins,
family that never could be loved more.
I don't want euphemisms for your names.
I don't want anyone to speak
your names.

I ask for a second, a century of peace
and remembrance for all
the dead Jewish women,
the Gypsy women,
the women of Bosnia.
They are all named
Julia, Silvia, Sonia,
and they are mine.
At our places at all the major holidays,
before saying the blessing,
we named them.

—Translated from Spanish by Stephen A. Sadow and J. Kates

PEACE

Don't fear the nearness of death.
You saw it pass by that night
When the daisies turned the color of shadows.
You saw it when you came down with your face over the balustrade
And the invisible angel of life protecting you.

Now the days and nights pass without calendars.
Lost in time
You have come to an agreement with the forgotten.
You inhabit a well of clear water
Where alone the dreams guide you
Disoriented over the days.

I play with your hair and in it I find
Brooches of garnet in the silvered locks.
I kiss your hands and you recognize me.
Your hair shines and your face shines.
You are safe,
Not even death can find you here.

—Translated from Spanish by Stephen A. Sadow and J, Kates

Ruth Behar

Ruth Behar (1955–), anthropologist and author, is the Victor Perrera Distinguished University Professor of Anthropology at the University of Michigan. Born in Havana, Cuba, she has lived in Spain and Mexico and returns often to Cuba to build bridges around culture and art. She is a MacArthur Fellow, a Carnegie Corporation Great Immigrant, and a member of the American Academy of Arts and Sciences. Her acclaimed scholarly books include *The Presence of the Past in a Spanish Village* (1986), *Translated Woman* (1993), *The Vulnerable Observer* (1996), *An Island Called Home* (2007), and *Traveling Heavy* (2013). Other works include a bilingual book of poems, *Everything I Kept / Todo lo que guardé* (2018), a documentary, *Adio Kerida* (2002), the prize-winning young adult novels *Lucky Broken Girl* (2017) and *Letters from Cuba* (2019), and a children's book on Sephardic Cuban heritage, *Tía Fortuna's New Home* (2022).

DREAM OF SEFARAD

Depart and never return
They told us

Forget about Spain
They told us

Do not dare to live in any of our cities, towns, and villages
They told us

Under penalty of death
They told us

Banished, you are banished from all our kingdoms
They told us

We have made quince jam from the fruit of the trees
We have drunk the wine from the sweet grapes
We have bathed in these rivers
We have welcomed with our faith the new moon
We have loved, brought up our children, buried our dead in this red earth
We have written poems in Hebrew, Arabic, Castilian
We have built modest synagogues, nothing comparable to your cathedrals
We have recited prayers for peace with our souls as open as the sea
We have wished for a *mazal bueno* to those who surrendered to your Cross

We have been here for more than a thousand years, generation upon generation

We have put down roots so deep, how can we leave this soil?
Cities with such beautiful names—
Toledo, Barcelona, Segovia, Zamora, Córdoba

Pretend you won't remember us
Pretend you won't miss us
Pretend you won't see us lurking in the shadows

Sefarad is our home, Spain is our Sefarad
Who are you to take Sefarad and Spain from us?

Weep for my people, who are shutting the doors and clasping the keys
Weep for my people, who are filling the boats at the port of Cádiz
Weep for my people, who are sweating in the damp heat of summer
Weep for my people, who are carrying the Torah on their shoulders
Weep for my people, who are glancing back, seeing only a Moor wave goodbye
Weep for my people, who are bemoaning their lives, wishing only to die
Weep for my people, who are going forth into another exile
Weep for my people, who are furious for having loved Sefarad so much
Weep for my people, who are wondering if Sefarad was only a dream

Many autumns have passed
Look—
Already my people are drying their tears
Already my people are bowing to another shore
Already a cry rises from my people:
I won't weep anymore
I won't weep anymore

Hijica, hear the song inside our hearts
It's sweet and sad and beautiful and broken
It's all that we kept:
the nostalgia for the sad breeze of Spain.

—Translated from Spanish by the author

PRAYER

This happens to me often, too often: I am on my way home, driving down familiar streets, only a few blocks to go, and out of nowhere a merciless hand comes and grips my heart and wrings it dry. I tremble. Fog clouds my eyes. I am no longer sure if I am awake or dreaming. If I die, who will find me? All I can do is pray: Let me return home, I am almost there, please. . . .

I don't know why this happens. What I know is that, so far, my prayers have been answered. Hardly breathing, I reach my house. And when I open the door, I hear many keys clanging, the keys my ancestors stubbornly took with them to their exile.

—Translated from Spanish by the author

Daniel Chirom

Poet, journalist, and attorney Daniel Chirom (1955–2008) was born in Buenos Aires. He published numerous books of poetry, among them *Crónica a Robledo Puch* (1975), *Los Atlantes* (1979), *La Diáspora* (1983), and *El hilo de oro* (1989). Chirom won first prize from the Inca Poetry Foundation with his poetry collection *Candelabros,* later published in 2000. He edited the *Antología de la nueva poesía Argentina* (1980) and anthologies of Walt Whitman, Wallace Stevens, and Raúl Gustavo Aguirre. He was director of the illustrated poetry magazine *El Jabalí* and a radio program with the same title. Chirom was deeply moved by the car bombing of the AMIA building in 1994.

JULY 19

Why is this night different from all other nights?
On all other nights we eat in abundance
and we sing and laugh over the wine,
but tonight we have only unleavened bread and vinegar
because we are sad, thinking about exile.
Why on this night do we not intone canticles?
Every night we praise God
as beautifully as we can,
but this night
silence reigns
because we have lost our appetite
and the desert is vast.
Why on this night do shadows take possession of our houses?
On all other nights lights illuminate the table,
but tonight there is only one candelabra
so that we remember darkness.
Why on this night do our hands and tongues tremble?
On all other nights we pray for the day to come
and we dance at the foot of our bed
because innocent blood does not leave footprints.
But tonight we stay quiet
while the waters flow down,
and our prayers are for the dead
who still accompany us.
Why on this night do we keep our mouths closed and shut our eyes?
On all other nights words protect us from stone,
but tonight the voices are mute
and we laugh in tragic joy
as a solitary wall betrays our lack of shelter.
Why on this night does everyone hide his face?

On all other nights we praise our comrades
and with eloquence we keep
bodies from falling,
but tonight the absence
injures our old flesh
and the solitude of the name
makes us listen to what we saw before.
Why on this night did joy fold its wings
and silence deflect our thoughts?
On all other nights, even when death
steps on our heels,
we tell the phases of the moon and praise the lion.
But tonight nobody called at our door
and it is already too late for someone to come
and guide us through the stars.
Why is this night different from all other nights?
On all other nights a spirit soars,
our wedding day, imagine the first kiss,
the sudden splendor, the crazy beauty,
but tonight a frozen wind stains our faces
and our souls are dust and mud under the claws of lost memory.
On this night we are dogs who have strayed from our master.
On this night there is no one in the tomb.

—Translated from Spanish by Stephen A. Sadow and J. Kates

* July 19 is the night after the bombing of the AMIA Jewish Community Center in Buenos Aires

FOR MY DAUGHTER MAGDALENA

No, put no faith in
the word spoken in obligation,
attempting the adventure of life is useless
if it doesn't rise from the heart.
No, don't grumble
about your half-hearted inexperience,
innocence is the only thing that will keep you going through storms.
No, do not ask
baseless questions of the night,
it has answers only for the desperate.
No, do not listen
to insolent voices
fearing the unknown,
your quest is the essence of what you are.
Do not say no
to life.
It is the only one who has a right of refusal.
You are the day and the night,
the sun and the moon,
and everything that happens to you happens to the universe.
You are the prism through which the dead return.

—Translated from Spanish by Stephen A. Sadow and J. Kates

Myriam Moscona

Poet, novelist, translator, and journalist Myriam Moscona (1955–) was born in Mexico City of Bulgarian Sephardic parents. Her book-length poetry sequence *Negro marfil / Ivory Black* (2011) was published in bilingual form, with a translation from Spanish by Jen Hofer. Hofer's work received the Harold Morton London Translation Award from the Academy of American Poets and the PEN Translation Prize in 2013. Moscona is the author of *Los visitantes* (1989), *El árbol de los nombres* (1992), *El que nada* (2006), *Tela de sevoya* (2012), *La muerte de la lengua inglesa* (2020), *Ansina* (2015), which was written entirely in Ladino, and *León de Lidia* (2022). Moscona is the recipient of numerous awards, including the Prize of Aguascalientes, a Guggenheim Fellowship, and the Xavier Villaurrutia Prize.

WORTH DYING FOR

rabbi ben izmir said:
if you set your tongue on fire
        and the tongue doesn't burn
if you set your tongue in water
        and your tongue remains stolid
if you set your tongue to the wind
        and your tongue doesn't move
thus you have a holy tongue
        worth dying for

—Translated from Ladino by Ilan Stavans

WHAT WAS

those dusts
brought these muds
and these clouds
brought
these rains
and these rains
brought these colds
and these colds
brought this ice
and this ice brought
illness
and those dusts
are what they were
which are these words
        that will be no more

—Translated from Ladino by Ilan Stavans

Perla Schwartz

Mexican poet and essayist Perla Schwartz (1956–2019) studied journalism at the Carlos Septién García School, where she later taught. She was a commentator for the TV program *Para gente grande*. This poem deals with the massacre of protesters during the Olympic Games in Mexico City in 1968.

HOLOCAUST OF THE SOUL

The riddled bodies
are pierced by
a disarray of evanescent smoke:
the fire of the Holocaust of the Soul.
Scattered crystals
trapped by ashes,
night-grief
grieving nights.
October 2, 1968:
night that won't resign itself
to ending.
Night of blood encircled
by a clock without hands.
Graffiti of human sacrifice.
An angry God
Tlatelolco:
suppressed shout . . . buried shout
that bursts and crashes
against the urban wall.
The fire of the Holocaust of the Soul.
Total impunity
totting up
the sway of clamor and voices,
crown of fire
that persists tattooed
on the folds of the heart.

—Translated from Spanish by Stephen A. Sadow and J. Kates

Gerardo Lewin

Born in Buenos Aires, Gerardo Lewin (1955–) received a master's degree in theater from Tel Aviv University. He has translated from Hebrew works by Yossi Birstein, Yitzhak Orpaz, Etgar Keret, Reuven Miran, Alex Epstein, David Vogel, Tal Nitzan, Dan Tsalka, and Amos Oz. He is the author of *Amores muertos* (2003). In 2007 Lewin founded a blog of translations of Hebrew poetry entitled *From Here and There, Now and in the Past.*

GOLEM

Everything they told you
until this instant . . .
I could create you
with a little earth.
Of course: words.
These days, what do words matter?
I could create you with a simple spell.
I will see you wake up
as if after a voyage
in the silence of your gray eyes.
I would make you happy.
I want to say: I would have you smiling,
loved and peaceful.
And you need nothing or no one,
like a hidden stone.
And I will love you so
that I will guzzle my life in a second,
like a tear furrowing your face,
like honey surging from your breast.
Years will pass
and you will still be beautiful.
I will breathe into your mouth
four final letters.
You will die thanking me
for everything
they told you
until that instant.

—Translated from Spanish by Stephen A. Sadow and J. Kates

Andrés Bohoslavsky

Andrés Bohoslavsky (1960–) was born in Argentina. He worked on ships for years and rarely went ashore. His poetry collections are *El ghetto de Vincent* (2001), *El río y otros poemas* (2003), *El pianista gato negro y otros poemas* (2004), *Una noche en el bosque-poesía y otros poemas* (2014), *Los ojos de Sasha: o El final de un sueño rojo* (2017), *Medianoche en la plaza de sueños* (2021), and *El mundo es un poema inconcluso* (2023). Bohoslavsky's poetry is known for its irony, surprising juxtapositions, and unexpected commentaries.

UNCLE SERGUEY

Anyone who has a continuous smile on his face conceals a toughness that is almost frightening.

—GRETA GARBO

A ship brought my mother and her brother Serguey to New York
at the beginning of the last century.
Together with them, a married couple named Demsky disembarked.
Her own ideas turned her into a leader of the Russian immigrants.
Expelled by the immigration authorities,
she had seventy-two hours to abandon the country of liberty
and left for Argentina in another ship filled with poor people.
Her brother's hunger and instinct for survival
brought him to Hollywood,
where he made films with that other couple's son:
Issur Danielovitch Demsky, better known as Kirk
Douglas.
In Buenos Aires, she continued to pay with persecutions
for her way of thinking
while my uncle became a millionaire and, with the passing of time,
the owner of several jewelry stores.
This photo of us together, crumpled by the years,
in a city I don't recognize,
shows an impeccably organized man in a black suit.
My mother, at his side, dressed simply,
her hair done up with a comb and a flower, a rose
pinned on her jacket
as a symbol of the militants of her time.
Uncle Sergey's sons expanded their father's business,
adding more jewelry stores, a movie studio,
a fashion house and a real estate firm

that dominated rental properties here.
I earned my living in ships and shipyards,
traveled the world, even after my mother's death,
fixing the motors of the Atlantic trade
until airplanes finished them off and my work with them.
On shore for a few days in New York one time—how strange—
I came across campaign posters with Uncle Sergey's face,
a candidate for state senator, a giant picture repeated over and over
again
on the streets, with his eternal smile, overwhelming and insufferable.
And how much worse when I saw that red rose in his lapel.

—Translated from Spanish by Stephen A. Sadow and J. Kates

Sonia Chocrón

Born in Caracas, Venezuela, Sonia Chocrón (1961–), a poet, TV writer, and screenwriter, holds a degree from the Andrés Bello National University. Since 1987 she has published in newspapers with international circulation and magazines dealing with poetry, criticism, and fiction. She has also collaborated with many cultural and literary publications. Chocrón is considered a leading Venezuelan poet. Among her books of poetry are *Toledana* (1992), *Púrpura* (1998), *La buena hora* (2002), *Falsas apariencias* (2004), *La virgin del baño turco* (2008), *Hermana pequeña* (2020), and *Carnet de identidad* (2023). Her novel is entitled *Las mujeres de Houdini* (2012).

EXTREMELY PURE

(Kashrut)
Brown the onion make the dream brighter
prepare supper for your hungry man
drain the blood and soak the meat
in water that cleans the impurity
from the rancid bodies and its flies
add two flowers and serve yourself whole
naked and sweaty
that safe white bed
all is salt

—Translated from the Spanish by Stephen A. Sadow and J. Kates

A BODY IS AN ISLAND

A body is a house is an island
A body is an almost hermetic house
abandoned to the idea of itself
It is also an island that has been born
at midnight without furious tremors,
clearly alone, helpless,
exiled, separated from this world
A body is a house is a deserted island
with the thirst for the shape of the dust

—Translated from Spanish by Stephen A. Sadow and J. Kates

CARACAS

The order is to leave quickly
with the little girls of our eyes
with the flowers stabbed in the throat
to keep them from shouting.
And to save the holy scriptures
the places already in ashes
the dead the parks the pets
for when we turn back
from fear.

—Translated from Spanish by Stephen A. Sadow and J. Kates

Ilan Stavans

Ilan Stavans (1961–) was born in Mexico into a Yiddish-speaking household. He lived in Spain, England, and the Middle East before settling in New York. He is an essayist, cultural commentator, linguist, translator, journalist, actor, editor, publisher of Restless Books, and teacher. The following excerpt is from his award-winning, English-language, book-length poem *The Wall* (2019), which explores the ubiquity of walls in human history. It compares the journey of a father and son from Central America to that of the biblical Abraham and Isaac. To compose the volume Stavans traversed the US-Mexico border from one end to the other.

FROM *THE WALL*

Isaac's father
is
taking him
to the top.
The
fence
is
called
Moriah.
Call
it
terram visionis.
Or
Marwah,
which
is
in Mecca.
Or
call
it
Reja de Satanás,
where
a
sign
reads:
"Más
sabe
el
diablo
por

viejo
que
por
diablo."
How
easy
is
it
to
judge
wrongly
after
whatever
good
comes
from
judging
rightly?
"Where are we going?"
the boy asks.
"The Lord
has
announced
to me
this road,"
the father
responds.
"He wants
our
deliverance.
We shall offer Him
a sacrifice.

A lamb will satisfy Him."
Isaac,
seven years old,
smiles.
Father and son
climb
at night.
The desert
is
never
still:
if you're quiet,
you
might
hear the wind;
if you're alert,
you
might
see
the moon's
dress
in
all
its
splendor.
"Once we're at the top,
I'll hold you tight,
me oyes?"
orders the father.
"Where is the sacrificial lamb?"
"The Lord giveth
and

the Lord taketh away.
The lamb waits for us at the top."
No guards.
The father pulls up his son, Isaac.
Once at the top,
the father
takes
a screwdriver
out
of his leather jacket.
It
will
help
loosen
the fence.
The moon
glitters,
its
reflection
multiplied
on
the apathetic steel.
The father's left hand
chokes
the son—
"No
puedo
respirar, apá!"—
as
the right
hand
descends,

turning
the
fatal
screwdriver
into
a
rigorous
weapon.
STOP!
A sniper. Isaac's father
falls,
lifeless,
to the ground.
The boy
shrieks.
The
border patrol
asks
the boy
to climb
down:
DOWN.
"Where is the sacrificial lamb?"
inquires Isaac.
No,
the questions are:
Who is the Angel of Death?
and
Where is the Angel of Life?
Who saved Isaac?
and
From what?

Or better,
Did anyone
remember
to
save
the child?
Blood
spills
on
the ground,
a stream
from
the father's chest
onto
the cold cement.
Isaac
places
his
fingers
in it:
hot,
cold.

—Written in English by the author

Jenny Asse Chayo

Jenny Asse Chayo (1963–) received a degree in Latin American literature from the Ibero-American University in Mexico City and studied Jewish philosophy at the Hebrew University in Jerusalem. Her collections of poetry include *Busco en mi carne el nombre* (1997), *Es sed de morir el paraíso* (2005), *El tránsito de la luz* (2007), and *Leer el infinito* (2016), republished in English as *Reading the Infinite* (2020). In her poetry she explores traditional Jewish themes, such as the nature of God, man, and the written word; faith; light and darkness; wandering in the wilderness; exile; life in the Diaspora; return and redemption.

THE BOOK CAN ONLY BE WRITTEN AROUND THE BOOK

The book can only be written around the book.
Everything was created from time out of memory.
We have inherited the responsibility to give names.
"I prefer to keep quiet."
"If you keep quiet, things stay in their savage state,
there will be nothing to hold them in."
The Adamic word contained the essence of things.
"Adam, by naming, found imperfection.
The imperfection of sharing the named,
scarcity of the other,
the gap is always love."

—Translated from Spanish by Stephen A. Sadow and J. Kates

GOD IS HOSPITABLE

He weaves an invisible thread into our names.
He narrates the story, having lost his voice.
He hides behind His Book, throbbing.

To read is to be broken into pieces.
To interpret the meaning of the Infinite.

—Translated from Spanish by Stephen A. Sadow and J. Kates

I TREMBLE BEFORE THE IMMENSITY OF THE POSSIBLE

I tremble before the immensity of the possible.
Every book goes along, illuminated by itself
in the track of the perpetual.
Words fight in the creating womb.
Each written word defeats another word.
Words fight among themselves to appear on the page,
that is their vanity.
"I don't want to give up any possibility of speaking."
"A thousand worlds were destroyed before this one could exist."
God himself had to choose among infinite possibilities.
"Shall he refuse to create a better world?"
"Many worlds throb in His interior, and he chose one.
And so, here we are, image and likeness."

—Translated from Spanish by Stephen A. Sadow and J. Kates

María Gabriela Mizraje

Born in Buenos Aires and the daughter of a Jewish father and a Catholic mother, María Gabriela Mizraje (1965–), scholar, poet, and playwright, was a professor at the University of Buenos Aires from 1989 until 1996, when she moved to the University of Palermo. Her books include *Argentinas de Rosas a Perón* (1999), *Norah Lange: Infancia y sueños de walkiria* (1995), and *Katherine S. Dreier: Cinco meses en la Argentina desde el punto de vista de una mujer, 1918 a 1919* (2015). She believes that her two traditions have made her more sensitive to cultural differences.

AND I SEE CAMELS

And I see camels
carrying wax balsam and myrrh
and I see camels
the sky has blinkered their eyes
I draw back the veils and walk
paths of *gueulá* of multiple
redemptions as sand
as nests
where the ashy wing flourishes
where all brilliance is in the future
and the camels
cross
the thousand-year route the precipice
sunflower of connected steps
steps foreseen living steps
the camels
drinking my dreams
and promising my hours
and dragging my memory
And I see camels
like stars floating in the infinite night
forelegs in the sands
of the desert
wheels in which the quietest music
turns into an eternal murmur
And I see camels
rest in caravan the vast dream
a golden perfume clings to the belly
of the wind that is later before now
and scatters the days

and gathers the hands
My camels
throw themselves on the sand
and I see more camels
under the sand
their bones shine like moons
that have turned the land toward the heavens
they watch together at the buried scrolls
the future of the world
that will not end
they pulsate with old signs of what exists
and their constant heartbeats wake me
The time to be their children will come
and a grammatical octave slowly
is meant to bring together the leaves of silence
is meant to reunite its points and its rules
its points and its peaks its mysteries
The camels exist
(they have never left)
What they carry is meant to return
balsam and myrrh
and a wax
that illuminates and creates universe

—Translated from Spanish by Stephen A. Sadow and J. Kates

LAMENTATIONS

Lamentations of desolate Jeremiah
(alone with his God—that was already enough)
a stone cuts into him many stones
but he folds his hands and hurls at us
the immense prophecy the ineffective gesture
knowing himself wept over
by all the eloquence of the poets
by all the vaulted visions of the mystics
by every form of truth that risks
his fleeting splendor
until the end of eons
and silence.

—Translated from Spanish by Stephen A. Sadow and J. Kates

Jacqueline Goldberg

Born in Maracaibo, Zulia, in Venezuela, Jacqueline Goldberg (1966–) received a doctorate from the Central University of Venezuela. She is the author of poetry, children's literature, reportage, essays, visual arts criticism, food journalism, and testimonials. Her books include *Verbos predadores: Poesía reunida 2006/1986* (2007), *Las horas claras* (2012), and *Nosotros, los salvados* (2015). In 2013 she won Book of the Year from the Venezuelan Booksellers for *Las horas claras*. Goldberg has written extensively about the Holocaust.

POETICS

Suddenly the poet's mouth is overwhelmed by larvae,
such is the lightness.

One must extract them one by one
for the poem to return to its cause,
for the maelstrom of wounds to acquiesce.

The stabbed shrieks have been too many,
and also the persistence of funeral rites.

The forehead kisses the ground.
Happiness is no longer a daily affiliation.

Once the last fortune is rooted out,
the poem will need to be cut down to size,
like teeth, in a voracious trance.

The poem will grow from its own forgiveness,
offering cruxes, efforts, voyages. Leveled by a certain slavery.

And pain?
Will it need to be recovered so a book can grow within the book?
For the gash of a future tear?

To write, once more, is to exist in gloom, in the preterit,
abundant to the end.

—Translated from Spanish by Ilan Stavans

José Luis Fariñas

Born in Havana, José Luis Fariñas (1972–) is an internationally known painter, drawer, and aquarellist. His work is complex, highly detailed, and often hermetic; it is influenced by Albrecht Dürer, Hiëronymus Bosch, and Rembrandt. He studied at the Advanced School of the Arts. Fariñas is a member of the Union of Writers and Artists of Cuba and a member of the International Writers and Artists Association. His artworks are held by museums in the United States, Germany, and Spain. Fariñas illustrated special editions of *Don Quixote* and the writings of Luis de Carvajal the Younger. Old Testament images frequently appear in his art. His poetry, published in Cuban journals, contains hidden references to the Kabbalah.

BRIEF INTRODUCTION TO NOTHINGNESS

The infinite sustains its exiles,
its chapters in expansion
—and there is no ultimate limit,
ultimate moment, nor ultimate being.
The turmoil embodies its boundaries deferred.
—JUANA GARCÍA ABÁS

I

They don't know if by tasting them, they will win the other light
or the impenetrable faith that created oblivion
with its bereaved judges
behind the seven or more seals about to open.
The wisest—or the most impatient—leans toward the fruits
and tastes, with an unexpected trembling,
the inner surfaces of such a strange risk.
They still believe themselves to be unprepared for the sacrifice;
in that consists of their innocence.

II

They seem to covet renunciation,
but something more severe pushes them.
Their mouths are closed
and their postures reflect the extraordinary cold
that burns what is not manifest:
they are passing through the definitive and inaccessible name.

III

Layer upon layer, the first face of God is discovered,
with simplicity, between lines of oil and pigments
that bind the curvatures of the unrevealed
until allowing it to appear through the fabric of the ancient waters.
The image is the only certainty, the artifice of salvation.

IV

Life and death melt down their wheels.
The newest is the oldest.
The furthest away, the nearest.
And no possibility remains
without spinning its disks and or rolling
on top of cathedrals and legions
their counted stones,
among those that the father and son seek for the sacrifice.

—Translated from Spanish by Stephen A. Sadow and J. Kates

REQUIEM

Flesh of silence.
Scarcely the root that is no more.
Psalms that spin and explode
against decrepit walls.
We suffer until we melt away like prayer
where dragonflies glide,
in the light of labyrinths that reflect dead skies.
Here we were, timber of return.
Psalms that return and cross
and dissolve like crystals of ice
at the doors of the oven.

—Translated from Spanish by Stephen A. Sadow and J. Kates

David Preiss

David Preiss (1973–) was born in Santiago, Chile, and received his doctorate in psychology at Yale University. He is a professor at the Pontifical Catholic University of Chile, where he conducts research on the psychology of writing and the psychology of creativity. His poetry books include *Señor del Vértigo* (1992/1994), which received an honorable mention in the Santiago Literature Prize in 1993, *Y demora el Alba* (1995), and *Lengua materna* (2020). David Preiss has received fellowships from the Pablo Neruda Foundation and the National Council on Books and Reading. He is a leader in the movement against anti-Semitism in Chile.

SON OF THE PACT

I didn't choose this pact.
But its memory begins
the day when my father,
in agreement with my mother,
decided to mark me
with a transparent wound
in the middle of the city
besieged by the tanks.
It is 1973. You
will be a Latin American
Jew, an oxymoron
that lives and breathes.
You will speak a language
that is not yours, you will inhabit
a transitory homeland,
you will be a stranger
among your own:
they will hate and they will love you.

My memory runs away,
flies, and stops
in San Cristobal, Venezuela.
It slowly settles
in improvised synagogues
where a minyan
of forgotten Jews
celebrated the Days of Awe
in the tropical Andes.
The chazzan asked forgiveness for the sins
that we committed and that we didn't commit

in a language brought from the ghettos
while the children escaped
from death and from his voice,
exploring attics
in an uncharted future:
as little Ulysses,
they challenged imaginary sirens,
far away from his god.

Instead of that ancient Hebrew,
my memory learns Spanish
with the Hispanic-
American ABC and reads the postcards
arriving from Maule
or from an always grim Santiago:
it was my grandma's handwriting
entrusting me to the Messiah
already denied by my parents,
dispatching with its invisible crosses
the pictures of high peaks, cold seas,
the snow that my childhood imagined
in the middle of the tropics,
the ports and the rural plazas
with children and doves
and chinchinero drummers, images
of a faceless country
where things were happening
that my grandma didn't share
and that entered and exited
the nightmares of my father
and my mother as the wind
enters and exits
a house whose

guests
suddenly withdrew.

In San Cristobal, my memory runs into
the jokes about Chile
made by my schoolmates
—how ugly that country was,
its mountains falling
into the sea.
Against them, my memory collects
clay figurines and copper crafts
and embroidery woven by the women of Chile
and little flags, lots of little flags,
and listens to my parents'
talk about returning, when to return.

But my memory moves away
from my imaginary homeland
and crosses the Williamsburg Bridge
in a subway train covered with graffiti
—a train, always the sound of the rail—
along with Jews, Blacks, and Latinos,
heading to Brooklyn
among the humid summer voices
and incomprehensibly familiar
Yiddish sounds.

In the apartments of the city
it finds
my bubbe's hands
buried in the flour
of gigantic challas

while my *tzaide* jokes
and sings with my father
old melodies
carried from a Europe
already sacrificed
over plastic tablecloths
stained with Manischewitz wine
and wax from the candles
that, like the martyrs' lives,
never end extinguishing
and that we can't blow out with just a sigh:
it's the same fire
I have used to mark and to celebrate
behind every Christmas
eight times each time
the Festival of Lights
while I leave in my window
against the southern summer
an old candelabra.

My memory goes up and down
from forgotten planes,
sky racers that the twentieth century
has devoured, and it stays
forever in return
walking toward the altar
between heaven and earth,
carrying the Torah,
—how its heavy
words weighed
on my arms—
under the stained glass

illuminated
by the spring light
in the Great Synagogue of the Israelite
Circle of Santiago
—Serrano and Tarapaca—
where it renews its pact
in front of a few survivors
that could never forget: it was
the first of November, Day
of the Dead—nineteen
eighty-six—while outside
they were killing
for thirteen years as well.

To my parents

—Translated from Spanish by Stephen A. Sadow with David Preiss

Leandro Sarmatz

Born in Porto Alegre, Brazil, and a descendant of Jewish immigrants who arrived in Rio Grande do Sul in the 1920s, Leandro Sarmatz (1973–) has lived in São Paulo since 2001. He edits the journal *Todavia*. He is a journalist, writer, and playwright whose books include the poetry collection *Logocausto* (2009), the short story collection *Uma fome* (2010), and the set of novellas *Ariel, Quixote do Holocausto & Carmen Cohen* (2018). In 2010 he wrote the play *Mães e sogras*. Sarmatz's poetics is sophisticated, marked by formal mastery and the use of exaggeration and, at times, parody.

YEHUDAH HALEVI

Beyond the door and behind the city lie
eras, generations, points on the compass.

There inside, the roofs and cupolas
reflect the scarce light of the end of the day.

Think: Sepharad remained in some place,
in another part, in other half,

in the east and not in the east, in the land
and in the streams and in the gold. Here is the east.

In some point in Europe, evasive
daughter, who at the edge of the abysm

blinks the eyes and arranges the braids,
someone or something, man, plant,

animal, or stone, sleeps and goes on,
dying covered up with snow or grief.

Not here: there is sun and good truth,
sun all at will, sun beating down

that fades the leaves, dries the life,
darkens the skins, fries the highest place.
But it is his sun. Adonai. Sun
that there hangs stationary all day.

A sun that he seeks and finds,
but in the end (recalcitrant Moses)
is not able to turn the hourglass,
and falls to the edge of the door to the city.

It dies. Before that, he calls out to the sorrowful gray
God, that cloud, that emptiness, that death.

—Translated from Portuguese by Regina Igel

A TOAST

Ruins of me,
always waiting,
for the false Messiah
and the day when
grief will cover
the bride without a veil
and a head without the kippah.
In a bright January,
on the contrary—ritual,
habit, or mania,
I will raise a goblet,
cut the bread, and announce
(smile and toothpaste):
the destruction of the temple,
the bloodied children,
the chimney,
the exile,
a page of a book.

—Translated from Portuguese by Regina Igel

Andrés Neuman

Andrés Neuman (1977–) was born in Buenos Aires, where he spent his childhood. The son of Argentine Jewish émigrés, he lives in Granada, Spain. He has a degree in Spanish philology from the University of Granada, where he taught Latin American literature. The author of numerous novels, short stories, poems, aphorisms, and travel books, he was selected as one of *Granta*'s Best of Young Spanish-Language Novelists. *Traveler of the Century* (2010), his first novel translated into English, won the National Critics Prize. His collection of short stories *The Things We Don't Do* (2015) won the Firecracker Award for fiction, given by the Community of Literary Magazines and Presses with the American Booksellers Association. Neuman's works have been translated into twenty-two languages.

GENESIS, COVID-19

And the Pope said amen in the empty square
and no one answered from the clouds
and no one answered from the mirrors
because all voices were beneath the ground
sweetly cradled to cease existence.
And the Stock Exchange swelled its lung
and counted the oxygen in coins
and rerouted its wind toward some islands
sewn to the sea with sutured wounds
only for lizards and exceptions.
And all countries became one
but specially themselves
since many needed to choose
between virus and bread and a few saved
a piece of future in the freezer.
And supermarkets were crowded
with animals in search of animals
with families in white that grazed
in a field of alcohol paper and plastic
and gloves keying the fear code.
And each hospital became tempest
and roofs rained and doors flew
and the thread of life became clear-cut
and truth came and went in hallways
without being asked any questions.
And grandparents could see
with skin like fishing nets
and hands stained with memory
and eyes blinded by lucidity
their rights turn into numbers.

And technology was flesh
in those who already had it and ghost
in those with only body
and we sang rhyming songs
promising never to forget.
And very soon our voices went quiet
in the usual places in multiple corners
with a fly's buzz in that devil's limbo
which is the border between song and silence
between mourning and amnesia.

—Translated from Spanish by Ilan Stavans

Sigalit Tevet

An immigrant from Chile to Israel at an early age, Sigalit Tevet (1984–) was raised in Tel Aviv and studied engineering at Tel Aviv University. She works in Botswana in the solar-energy industry. Tevet translates Chilean poetry into Hebrew.

WHO IS ACCOUNTABLE?

On the 10th of Av,
a white Renault Trafic van,
carrying a bomb
made of 275 kilograms
of ammonium nitrate fertilizer
and fuel oil explosive mixture,
explodes in Buenos Aires
at the AMIA.
Who is accountable?
It is 9:53 a.m.
85 die,
including Jorge Antúnez,
who is just finishing 7th grade.
And
Leonor Gutman de Finkelchtein,
with her daughter
Ingrid Finkelchtein,
who are
waiting for Ingrid's friend,
Carla Andrea Josch,
and her sister,
Analía Verónica Josch.
Did they meet?
Ricardo Said,
who guards the entrance to the building,
won't witness his daughter
recite Canto I of *The Gaucho Martín Fierro*
that evening at a poetry competition:
"Aquí me pongo a cantar . . ."
There are 300 people injured,

among them Tía Consuelo,
whose ears will explode as well
and shall never pick up
my phone calls again.
The echoes are too remote.
Who is accountable?
The bombing is retaliation against Israel:
we have killed
—shamelessly—
our ever-growing share of enemies.
But is Calle Pasteur #633
in Tel Aviv?
In Sidon, Lebanon,
leaflets are distributed by Ansar Allah,
a Jihadist organization,
claiming responsibility.
A Hezbollah operative
is honored with a plaque
declaring him a martyr.
Abraham Jaime Plaksin
dies after preparing one of his classes
in the shul on Calle Libertad.
Jorge Mario Bergoglio,
the former Catholic Church cardinal
crowned Pope Francis,
signs a petition demanding justice
in the Vatican.
Justice?
Under what jurisdiction?
Mónica Nudel,
walking on Calle Pasteur
in search of merchandise,

thinks the soul needs fixing.
But who is accountable?
A memorandum of understanding,
part of "a truth commission,"
is signed,
yet no judge emits a sentence.
Officially Israel expresses solidarity,
and the White House
offers support in the investigation.
What is being sought?
Rita Worona,
in charge of funerals,
didn't plan her own burial.
Cristina Fernández de Kirchner,
Argentina's president,
faces charges
for covering up details
and for abuse of power.
Does anyone care?
The Mossad,
after a lengthy investigation,
concludes
that Iran didn't have
operatives on the ground.
Who is accountable?
A librarian won't catalog countless books
describing the tragedy.
What tragedy?
Alberto Nisman,
a federal prosecutor,
is found dead
a day before he is scheduled to report his findings

accusing Hezbollah of plotting the tragedy.
It is 9:53 a.m.
on July 18, 1994.
A bomb explodes,
but no one hears it.

—Translated from Hebrew by Ilan Stavans

Translators

CELESTE KOSTOPULOS COOPERMAN has translated several books by the Chilean American poet Marjorie Agosín, including *A Cross and a Star, An Absence of Shadows, Always from Somewhere Else*, and *Beyond the Time of Words*. She was awarded the Outstanding Translation Award from the American Literary Translation Association, and her translations of Latin American women's poetry have appeared in many literary journals.

COLA FRANZEN (1923–2018) translated a total of fifteen books by notable Spanish and Latin American authors, including Saúl Yurkievich, Jorge Guillén, Alicia Borinsky, Juan Cameron, and Antonio José Ponte, as well as *Poems of Arab Andalusia*. Franzen was awarded the 2004 Gregory Kolovakos Prize by PEN American Center.

ROBERTA GORDENSTEIN's translations include Luzmaría Jiménez Faro's *Beloved Angels* and poems and stories in the anthologies *The House of Memory: Stories by Jewish Women Writers of Latin America* and *Miriam's Daughters: Jewish Latin American Women Poets*. She is a former professor of Spanish at Elms College.

ALBERTO HUBERMAN is a member of the Mexican Academy of Science. He has received many prizes from national and international institutions. He was a founding member of kibbutz Gaash. He has translated Israeli literature as well as English authors.

Professor emerita of Brazilian and Portuguese literatures and cultures at the University of Maryland, REGINA IGEL is the author of *Imigrantes judeus / Escritores brasileiros: O componente judaico na literatura brasileira*. She is a contributing editor to the *Handbook of Latin American Studies*, a publication of the Library of Congress.

J. KATES is a minor poet and a literary translator. He is the translator of a dozen books of Russian and French poetry, has edited two anthologies of translations, and collaborated with Stephen A. Sadow on Spanish poetry in translation.

ELIEZER NOWODWORSKI was born in Argentina and lives in Israel. He studied history at Tel Aviv University and works as a translator and interpreter. His Spanish translations have been published in Spain, Argentina, Peru, and Mexico.

STEPHEN A. SADOW, alone and very often with J. Kates, has translated forty-five Latin American Jewish poets and Spanish poets from Spanish and Portuguese into English. He and J. Kates have translated book-length works by Ricardo Feierstein, Isaac Goldemberg, Juana García Abás, Jenny Asse Chayo, and Alicia Aza. Many of their translations have been published in literary magazines in the US, England, Ireland, Sweden, and Bangladesh.

MARK SCHAFER is a literary translator, a visual artist, and a senior lecturer at the University of Massachusetts in Boston, where he teaches Spanish. He has translated works by David Huerta, Belén Gopegui, Virgilio Piñera, and Alberto Ruy Sánchez, and most recently Gloria Gervitz's book-length *Migrations: Poem, 1976–2000*.

ILAN STAVANS is the Lewis-Sebring Professor of Humanities and Latin American and Latino Culture at Amherst College, the publisher of Restless Books, and a consultant to the *Oxford English Dictionary*. His translations of poetry, from many languages and featured in *Selected Translations: Poems, 2000–2020*, include works by Sor Juana Inés de la Cruz, Emily Dickinson, Jorge Luis Borges, Pablo Neruda, Elizabeth Bishop, Juan Gelman, Yehuda Amichai, and Richard Wilbur. Stavans has translated *Don Quixote, Alice in Wonderland,* and *The Little Prince* into Spanglish.

Poets in Alphabetical Order

Rubén Ackerman
Marjorie Agosín
Lucia Aizim
Moacir Amâncio
Jenny Asse Chayo
Ruth Behar
Andrés Berger-Kiss
Yitzkhok Berliner
Andrés Bohoslavsky
Leonor de Carvajal y Andrade
Luis de Carvajal the Younger
Sonia Chacrón
Daniel Chirom
Juana Ciesler
Sandro Cohen
Juan Bautista Corvera
Humberto Costantini
Ariel Dorfman
Sara Riwka B'raz Erlich
José Luis Fariñas
Ricardo Feierstein
Manuela Fingueret
Hjalmar Flax
Luisa Futoransky
Julia Galimare
Juana García Abás
Aída Gelbtrunk
Juan Gelman
Gloria Gervitz
Yankev (Jacobo) Glantz
Moishe Glikovski
Jacqueline Goldberg
Isaac Goldemberg
Miryam Gover de Nasatsky
Susana Grimberg
Carlos Grünberg
Irene Gruss
Raúl Hecht
Tamara Kamenzsain
Rosita Kalina
Jevel Katz
Luis Kleiman
Shloyme Kleinberg
José Kozer
Carlos Jacobo Levy
Gerardo Lewin
Lázaro Liacho
María Gabriela Mizraje
Miryam Moscona
Angelina Muñiz-Huberman
Andrés Neuman
Gonzalo Pérez Ferro
Moishe Pinchevsky
Alejandra Pizarnik
David Preiss
Arminda Ralesky

Becky Rubinstein F.
Daniel Samoilovich
Leandro Sarmatz
Perla Schwartz
Leonor Scliar-Cabral
Marcos Silber
Perla Sneh
Ilan Stavans
Nora Stejilevich
Sigalit Tevet
César Tiempo
Eliahu Toker
David Turkeltaub
Bella Clara Ventura
Evelyn Wertheimer
Héctor Yánover
Saúl Yurkievich
Simón Zeleviansky

Permissions

The editor gratefully acknowledges permission to reproduce the following material:

Juan Bautista Corvera (attributed): "Mileno vs. Apolindo." Adapted from Spanish by Ilan Stavans. Used by permission of the translator.

Leonor de Carvajal y Andrade: "For All Who Trust Him." Adapted from Spanish by Ilan Stavans. Used by permission of the translator.

Luis de Carvajal the Younger: "You, Without You." Adapted from Spanish by Ilan Stavans. Used by permission of the translator.

Gonzalo Pérez Ferro: "Shemá Israel." Translated from Spanish by Ilan Stavans. Used by permission of the translator.

Yitzhak Berliner: "Popocatépetl." Translated from Yiddish by Ilan Stavans. Originally published in *Selected Translations: Poems, 2000–2020* (University of Pittsburgh Press, 2021). Used by permission of the translator.

Shloyme Kleinberg: "In-Between Question." Translated from Yiddish by Ilan Stavans. Used by permission of the translator.

Moishe Pinchevsky: "Arriving Early." Translated from Yiddish by Ilan Stavans and Eliezer Nowodworski. Used by permission of the translators.

Jacobo Glantz: "The Meaning of My Life" and excerpt from *Kristobal Kolon*, Part II, Section 17. Translated from Yiddish by Ilan Stavans. Used by permission of the translator.

Jevel Katz: "Moisés Ville." Translated from Casteidish by Ilan Stavans. Originally published in *Jewish Review of Books* (Summer 2022). Used by permission of the translator.

Moishe Glikovski: "My Children." Translated from Yiddish by Ilan Stavans. Used by permission of the translator.

Carlos Grünberg: "Neo-Jews" and "HINTLER." Translated from Spanish by Stephen A. Sadow and J. Kates. Used by permission of Gabriela Grünberg and the translators.

César Tiempo: "Harangue on the Death of Chaim Nachman Bialik." Translated from Spanish by Stephen A. Sadow and J. Kates. Used by permission of the translators.

Lázaro Liacho: "To Be Born Jewish" and "Love." Translated from Spanish by Stephen A. Sadow and J. Kates. Used by permission of the translators.

Simón Zeleviansky: "By the River Plate." Translated from Yiddish by Ilan Stavans. Used by permission of the translator.

Lucia Aizim: "Wandering." Translated from Portuguese by Regina Igel. Used by permission of the translator.

Julia Galimare: "Poetic Diary I." Translated from Spanish by Stephen A. Sadow and J. Kates. Used by permission of the author and the translators.

Humberto Costantini: "I Point Out" and "My Job." Translated from Spanish by Stephen A. Sadow and J. Kates. Used by permission of Editorial Katun, Buenos Aires, and the translators.

Arminda Ralesky: "VI." Translated from Spanish by Stephen A. Sadow and J. Kates. Used by permission of the author and the translators.

Andrés Berger-Kiss: "I Do Not Want This Wound to Heal." Translated from Spanish by Stephen A. Sadow and J. Kates. Used by permission of Editorial Betania, Spain, and the translators.

Leonor Scliar-Cabral: "Shavuot in Granada" and "Sephirot." Translated from Portuguese by Regina Igel. Used by permission of the author and the translator.

Héctor Yánover: "Now" and "Cat, help the poet." Translated from Spanish by Stephen A. Sadow and J. Kates. Used by permission of Debora Yánover and the translators.

Juan Gelman: "End" and "Epitaph." Translated from Spanish by Ilan Stavans. First published in *The FSG Book of Twentieth-Century Latin American Poetry* (New York: Farrar, Straus, and Giroux, 2011). Used by permission of the heirs of Juan Gelman and the translator.

Juan Gelman: "Dibaxu: I." Translated from Ladino by Ilan Stavans. First published in *The FSG Book of Twentieth-Century Latin American Poetry* (New York: Farrar, Straus, and Giroux, 2011). Used by permission of the heirs of Juan Gelman and the translator.

Saúl Yurkievich: "Tumbles and Rumbles." Translated from Spanish by Cola Franzen. Used by permission of the heirs of the translator.

Raúl Hecht: "When You Open the Window." Translated from Spanish by Stephen A. Sadow and J. Kates. Used by permission of the author and the translators.

Marcos Silber: "I See Him - 1911." Translated from Spanish by Stephen A. Sadow and J. Kates. Used by permission of El Mono Armado Editores, Buenos Aires, and the translators.

Rosita Kalina: "I Am of the Tribe of Judah" and "To Transcend Life." Translated from Spanish by Stephen A. Sadow and J. Kates. Used by permission of Ileana Piszk and the translators.

Eliahu Toker: "Homage to My Jewish Condition." Translated from Spanish by Stephen A. Sadow and J. Kates. Used by permission of Corina Toker and the translators.

Sara Riwka B'raz Erlich: "Daughters of the Diaspora" and "Transazure." Translated from Portuguese by Regina Igel. Used by permission of the author and the translator.

Angelina Muñiz-Huberman: "The Kabbalists" and "The Eye of Creation." Translated from Spanish by Stephen A. Sadow and J. Kates. Used by permission of the author and the translators.

Angelina Muñiz-Huberman: "The Palace and Sepharad." Translated from Spanish by Ilan Stavans, with Angelina Muñiz-Huberman and Alberto Huberman. Used by permission of the author and the translators.

Angelina Muñiz-Huberman: "Passover." Translated from Spanish by Ilan Stavans. First published in *New World Haggadah* (Gaon Books, 2016). Used by permission of the author and the translator.

Alejandra Pizarnik: "Poem for the Father" and "Only." Translated from Spanish by Ilan Stavans. First published in *The Common* (April 2022). Used by permission of the estate of Alejandra Pizarnik and the translator.

Miryam Gover de Nasatsky: "Guard Tower." Translated from Spanish by Stephen A. Sadow and J. Kates. Used by permission of the author and the translators.

Luisa Futoransky: "Jerusa of My Love." Translated from Spanish by Stephen A. Sadow and J. Kates. Used by permission of the author and the translator.

David Turkeltaub: "Geratevet." Translated from Spanish by Stephen A. Sadow. Used by permission of Nina Turkieltaub and the translator.

Aída Gelbtrunk: "You Already Feel the Air Bearing Rain." Translated from Spanish by Stephen A. Sadow. Used by permission of the translator.

Aída Gelbtrunk: "All illusion is a form of hope." Translated from Spanish by Roberta Gordenstein. First published in *Miriam's Daughters: Latin American Jewish Women Poets* (Sherman Asher, 2001). Used by permission of the translator.

José Kozer: "Passover in Havana" and "Diaspora." Translated from Spanish by Stephen A. Sadow and J. Kates. Used by permission of the author and the translators.

Juana Ciesler: "His Brother Zalman." Translated from Spanish by Stephen A. Sadow and J. Kates. Used by permission of Beatriz Méndez and the translators.

Carlos Jacobo Levy: "*L'Chaim*" and "Ay, Antonio, once again once more but no." Translated from Spanish by Stephen A. Sadow and J. Kates. Used by permission of Julieta Levy and the translators.

Ricardo Feierstein: "Nationality," "Nostalgia," and "Distinguishing Characteristics." Translated from Spanish by Stephen A. Sadow and J. Kates. First published in *We the Generation of the Desert* (Ford Brown, 1989) and in *Las Edades* (The Ages) (Editorial Milá, 2004). Used by permission of the author and the translators.

Hjalmar Flax: "Tenacity." Translated from Spanish by Stephen A. Sadow and J. Kates. Used by permission of the author and the translators.

Ariel Dorfman: "VOCABULARY." Used by permission of the author.

Gloria Gervitz: excerpt from *Migrations*. Translated from Spanish by Mark Schaffer. Originally published in *Migrations: Poem, 1976-2020* (New York Review Books, 2021). Used by permission of Abe Maczka and the translator.

Isaac Goldemberg: "Inexact Sonnet of the Peruvian Jew and Vice Versa" and "Yom Kippur." Translated from Spanish by Stephen A. Sadow and J. Kates. First published in *Autorretratos y Mácaras* (Self-Portraits and Masks) (2002). Used by permission of the author and the translators.

Manuela Fingueret: "Second Portrait." Translated from Spanish by Roberta Gordenstein. First published in *Miriam's Daughters: Latin American Jewish Women Poets* (Sherman Asher, 2001) Used by permission of Luciano Dyzenchauz and the translator.

Manuela Fingueret: "Each Morning Making Sure." Translated from Spanish by Stephen A. Sadow and J. Kates. Used by permission of Luciano Dyzenchauz and the translators.

Evelyn Wertheimer: "of course the streets and the houses." Translated from Spanish by Stephen A. Sadow and J. Kates. Used by permission of the author and the translator.

Bella Clara Ventura: "Blind Faith." Translated from Spanish by Stephen A. Sadow and J. Kates. Used by permission of the author and the translators.

Tamara Kamenzsain: "I HAVE NEVER TOLD THIS to any of my analysts" and "SEATED AT THE EDGE OF her memory." Translated from Spanish by Stephen A. Sadow and J. Kates. Used by permission of Mauro Libertella and the translators.

Luis Kleiman: "III LOGIC." Translated from Spanish by Stephen A. Sadow and J. Kates. Used by permission of José Kleiman and the translators.

Becky Rubinstein F.: "Eve VI" And "Eve VIII." Translated from Spanish by Stephen A. Sadow and J. Kates. Used by permission of the author and the translators.

Daniel Samoilovich: "A Fable about the Origin of Man." Translated from Spanish by Stephen A. Sadow and J. Kates. Used by permission of the author and the translators.

Moacir Amâncio: "Saghi Nehor." Translated from Portuguese by Regina Igel. Used by permission of the author and the translator.

Irene Gruss: "Meanwhile." Translated from Spanish by Stephen A. Sadow and J. Kates. Used by permission of Irene Goldfarb and the translators.

Susana Grimberg: "First" and "Eve." Translated from Spanish by Stephen A. Sadow and J. Kates. Used by permission of the author and the translators.

Juana García Abás: "Testimony," "Textus," and "About Ordered Chaos." Translated from Spanish by Stephen A. Sadow and J. Kates. First published in *Sagrada arqueología* (Sacred Archeology) (Kindle, 2011). Used by permission of the author and the translators.

Nora Strejilevich: "When They Robbed Me of Name." Translated from Spanish by Celeste Kostopulos Cooperman. Originally published in *Miriam's Daughters: Latin American Jewish Women Poets* (Sherman Asher, 2001). Used by permission of the author and the translator.

Perla Sneh: "And he said to Abraham, send away that servant." Translated from Spanish by Stephen A. Sadow. Used by permission of the author and the translators.

Sandro Cohen: "This, in essence, ended . . ." Translated from Spanish by Stephen A. Sadow and J. Kates. Used by permission of Josefina Estrada and the translators.

Rubén Ackerman: "You Have to Turn the Page" and "Ars Poetica." Translated from Spanish by Stephen A. Sadow and J. Kates. Used by permission of Dcir Ediciones and the translators.

Marjorie Agosín: "Cousins" and "Peace." Translated from Spanish by Stephen A. Sadow and J. Kates. First published in *Miriam's Daughters: Latin American Jewish*

Women Poets (Sherman Asher, 2001). Used by permission of the author and the translators.

Ruth Behar: "Dream of Sefarad." Originally published in "Gestures of Memory: Seven Latin American/Latina Women Writers of Jewish Origin in the US," *Hostos Review* 14 (2017), and in *Caribbean Jewish Crossings*, University of Virginia Press, 2019. Used by permission of the author.

Ruth Behar: "Prayer." Originally published in *Everything I Kept / Todo lo que guardé* (Swan Isle Press, 2018). Used by permission of the author.

Daniel Chirom: "July 19" and "For My Daughter Magdalena." Translated from Spanish by Stephen A. Sadow and J. Kates. Used by permission of Aída Maltz and the translators.

Miryam Moscona: "Worth Dying For" and "What Was." Translated from Ladino by Ilan Stavans. Used by permission of the author and the translator.

Perla Schwartz: "Holocaust of the Soul." Translated from Spanish by Stephen A. Sadow and J. Kates. Used by permission of Jane Chertorivsky and the translators.

Gerardo Lewin: "Golem." Translated from Spanish by Stephen A. Sadow and J. Kates. Used by permission of the author and the translators.

Andrés Bohoslavsky: "Uncle Serguey." Translated from Spanish by Stephen A. Sadow and J. Kates. Used by permission of the author and the translators.

Sonia Chacrón. "Extremely Pure," "A Body is an Island," and "Caracas." Translated from Spanish by Stephen A. Sadow and J. Kates. Used by permission of the author and the translators.

Ilan Stavans: excerpt from *The Wall*. First published in *The Wall* (University of Pittsburgh Press, 2019). Used by permission of the University of Pittsburgh Press.

Jenny Asse Chayo: "The book can only be written around the book," "I tremble before the immensity of the possible," and "God is hospitable." Translated from Spanish by Stephen A. Sadow and J. Kates. First published in *Reading the Infinite* (Pendulum Press, 2016). Used by permission of the author and the translators.

María Gabriela Mizraje: "And I See Camels" and "Lamentations." Translated from Spanish by Stephen A. Sadow and J. Kates. Used by permission of the author and the translators.

Jacqueline Goldberg: "Poetics." First published in *Selected Translations: Poems 2000–2020* (University of Pittsburgh Press, 2021). Used by permission of the author and the translator.

José Luis Fariñas: "Brief Introduction to Nothingness" and "Requiem." Translated from Spanish by Stephen A. Sadow and J. Kates. Used by permission of the author and the translators.

David Preiss: "Son of the Pact." Translated from Spanish by Stephen A. Sadow and David Preiss. Used by permission of the author and the translator.

Leandro Sarmatz: "Yehudah HaLevi" and "A Toast." Translated from Portuguese by Regina Igel. Used by permission of the author and the translator.

Andrés Neuman: "Genesis, COVID-19." Translated from Spanish by Ilan Stavans. Originally published in *And We Came Outside and Saw the Stars Again: Writers on the COVID-19 Pandemic* (Restless Books, 2020). Used by permission of the author and the translator.

Sigalit Tevet: "Who Is Accountable?" Translated from Hebrew by Ilan Stavans. Used by permission of the author and the translator.

Index of Titles and First Lines